UNDERSTANDING GOOGLE APPS

A COMPREHENSIVE AND USEFUL GUIDE TO GOOGLE APPS FOR BEGINNERS AND EXPERTS

VICKY JOYCE

THE GOOGLE APPS

OVERVIEW

A web-based word processor and spreadsheet software, an email program, a WYSIWYG web editor, an online calendar, voice features for instant messaging clients, and more are all included in Google Apps, formerly known as Google Apps for your Domain. Google Apps are used by everyone, including individuals, businesses, and educational institutions. Without the Google Apps, the majority of people can essentially accomplish anything on the internet these days. These apps have made everyone's demands on the web more easily met. The good news is that Google Apps is available for free, although the premium version demands a fee. This has allowed small firms that cannot afford to hire IT specialists to manage their systems to expand, as Google Apps requires little to no technical knowledge. The components that make up Google Apps include a word processor, spreadsheet, email, and calendar. Because Google servers host these components, end users no longer have to deal with the inconvenience of installing and updating the software from their location. The ability for administrators to view and control user accounts via a web-based control panel sets this Google App apart. Compared to what Microsoft offers its consumers, Google Apps performs significantly better and is easier to use, particularly with Google Docs. This is just my personal perspective; you might feel differently about it. You need a web domain name in order to access the Google app because you cannot utilize it without one. Google recently announced a partnership with Registrars, including Go Daddy and eNom, to charge $10 annually for domain names. Google Apps are included with the domain name that you purchase straight from Google and don't need to be configured by the user.

There are two versions of Google Apps: the standard edition, often called the "free" edition, and the premier edition, also called the "paid" edition. Those who subscribe to the premier version receive 10GB of email storage, while those who use the free edition only receive 2GB. Additionally, a 99.9% email uptime guarantee is provided to Premier members. In addition, Premier subscribers can disable contextual ads on Google services and receive round-the-clock phone support. Additionally, they offer a number of cutting-edge features designed just for their business. The premier edition costs $50 per user account annually, so it's not cheap, but the perks it offers make up for the price, which many customers find satisfactory.

CHAPTER ONE
PRESENTING THE GOOGLE APPS

The majority of the things we do on a daily basis require access to the web since the world has gone digital. Approximately 80 to 85 percent of people utilize the internet for personal, professional, or educational purposes. It's almost impossible to find someone who hasn't heard of or used Google Apps. These days, internet connectivity has increased even in developing nations, to the point where nearly every developed and developing nation is aware of and uses Google Apps. Either you've used them already or you've heard about them. The internet is expanding in sophistication in tandem with the world's rotation.

Applications for word processing, spreadsheets, presentations, email reading, writing, and archiving, appointment scheduling, and meeting coordination are all included in Google Apps. Google Apps enabled online browser-based collaboration, productivity, and communication solutions. The fact that the majority of Google App programs are free to use is really intriguing. Word processing, spreadsheets, email, chat, Web page builder, and much more are available for free. In addition to the Google App's free version, there is a premium edition that you can purchase called the premier edition. Compared to the free edition, which only offers 2GB of email storage, the premier edition gives you more access to additional applications and 10GB of email storage. Additionally, a 99.9% email uptime guarantee is provided to elite users. In addition, the premium edition offers you the option to block contextual ads on Google services and round-the-clock phone support. You also receive customized advanced features for your business in addition to these. Whether it's the free version or the premier edition, the integrated Suite's offerings are exceptional. Aside from email, other Google applications include Google Maps, WYSIWYG web editors, instant messaging, and voice chat.

Employees may occasionally prefer to use a desktop mail client over Gmail's Ajax-based interface, such as Microsoft Outlook or Thunderbird. However, they can still utilize Gmail with their desktop software by utilizing POP access, one of the service's free features. Google Apps comes with a helpful program called Google Docs/spreadsheet. This tool has the power to transform how you compose and distribute papers to clients and coworkers. This resembles an online version of Excel or Word for Microsoft. Their interface features are similar to those of Microsoft software. The distinction is that documents must be created within a web browser, whereas Google Servers are used to store data online. The benefit is that any machine with an internet connection can access your papers.

It is stated that GTalk and Google Doc Spreadsheets are integrated. Google's instant messaging app is called The Talk. You may now access your documents from any location thanks to this. When they open the chat window, employees who are located in various places can update the same documents and spreadsheets concurrently. This allows people to quickly and in real time discuss and review modifications made by the firm or authors. The question of whether businesses will soon switch from Microsoft to Google Apps has been discussed. There is no denying that, based on what we currently observe from Google, Google App directly threatens Microsoft. Is that up to you to decide? The virtual collaboration tools available in Google Docs are significantly more extensive, better, and easier to use than those found in Microsoft Office apps at the moment. With regard to the most recent Microsoft Office apps, some businesses might not like their existing configuration. The fact that Google Apps lacks presentation-creation software in the form of PowerPoint is a drawback that keeps Microsoft ahead. The second drawback is that the Google server, which is located outside the organization's computers and storage system, houses all of the secret data for the company, including word and spreadsheet documents. Due to the disapproval of certain companies, this constraint exists.

Google Apps: What Are They?

The set of Google services and products known as Google Apps is made available to other organizations by Google.

The list of these goods and services is provided below;

- **Google Docs:** This tool allows you to create, modify, and share documents online for later offline editing whenever you'd like. You can create and work with word processors, spreadsheets, slide shows, and other types of documents that you can use in your presentation with Google Docs. With Google Docs, you can accomplish so much.

- **Gmail:** This email program file, which is based on the Google Web, gives you a lot of storage space. It also allows you to search and filter your emails at any time, and it's made to keep all of your messages organized.
- **Google Talk:** You can communicate with friends, family, and coworkers using this instant messaging service provided by Google. It is possible to find out who is online as well as when they are. You can initiate group chats with all of your online peers by sending them messages.
- **Calendar on Google.** You can now plan and schedule event management apps thanks to this. You are able to make many calendars with it. You may also use it to arrange events and share your calendars with friends, family, and coworkers so that everyone is aware of the global event.
- **Page Creator:** Using Page Creator and Google's web page editor, you may design and construct web pages and then publish them online for free.
- **Control Panel:** From here, Google App Administrators can alter every program used by their business and oversee each employee's personal account.
- **Start Page:** With the help of this program, you can create a unique home page with a start page for each person in an organization. You may also place your company's logo at the top with it. Announcements and the ability to add devices, such as mini-applications that you can place on a web page, are examples of this. This allows end users to access their Google Apps with just a single click. People are reminded to monitor their Gmail inboxes and their collection of crucial documents as a result. They can also use it to talk with their coworkers and check their appointments. You can personalize your start pages with the start page app to fit your tastes.
- **Google Websites:** With the help of this website, you may make collaborative webpages that numerous people can work on simultaneously, modify, and add material to.

Creating an account on Google

Signing up for a Google account has grown in popularity among PC and Android smartphone users. These days, almost everyone needs a Google account. In order to register for a Gmail account, you must first create a Google account, which is a quick process that will grant you a Gmail account name. In this part, you will learn how to set up your Gmail account on Google, add and change contacts, and modify email settings.

How To Set Up A Google Account

The steps given below must be followed in order to create a Google account. To make an account, navigate to www.gmail.com and click on the aforementioned website.

Simply follow the instructions when the signup form appears on the screen.

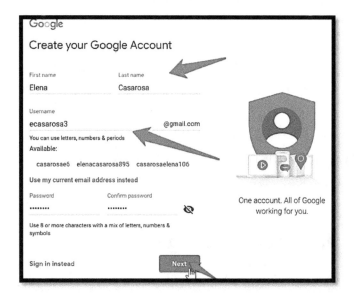

Entering your phone number will be the next step in the process to validate the account. For security purposes, a two-step verification process is required.

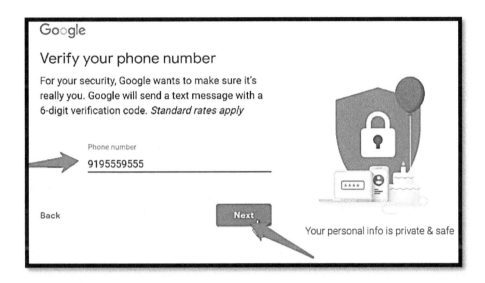

Google will send you a message with a verification code. Enter the code right away to complete the account verification without wasting time because it has limited time.

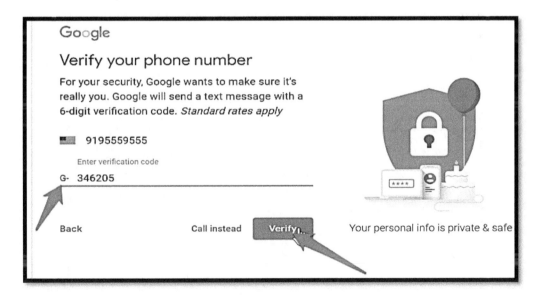

After clicking next, a form containing your name and birthday as well as other personal information will appear.

Reviewing your Google privacy and terms of service is required at this point. Once you've read it, click "I agree."

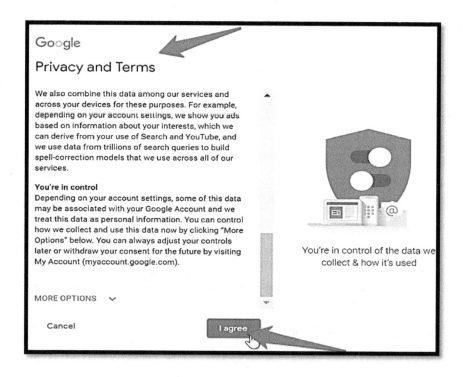

Your account has now been created and is prepared for use by you.

It is usually a good idea to come up with a strong password to prevent easy account access.

Logging Into Your Account

As soon as your account creation is complete, the system will log you into Gmail automatically. It is necessary for you to sign out, sign in again, then sign in again. It's also crucial that you consider logging out of Google Mail to be vital. This is due to the fact that since it's a public computer and the internet, someone else could take advantage of the chance to use your account and commit fraud in your name. Please sign out of the system and Gmail for security reasons.

Logging In

You must use the same website that you used to set up your Gmail account in order to log in. The website can still be accessed at www.gmail.com. As long as you can recall your email address and password, you can always access your email from any computer, tablet, or phone, no matter where you are in the globe. After entering your password and user name/email address, click the "Next" button.

Signing In

Your first initials are in a circle that you can see in the upper right corner of the website. Simply click the circle, then choose "Sign Out."

A Setting Change For Your Account

You are free to modify your Gmail account settings as needed; there are no issues with doing so. The alteration in behavior, look, or color is a matter of taste. People vary from one another in terms of their preferred color or appearance. Thus, you may choose to draft a vacation reply or a signature. Additionally, you can choose to modify your labels or, for example, alter your theme. When it comes to configuring your mail preferences, the choice is all yours. I'll walk you through the process of successfully changing your mail settings.

Getting Access To Your Settings For Email

You must look in the upper right corner of the display page and click Settings in order to view your email settings.

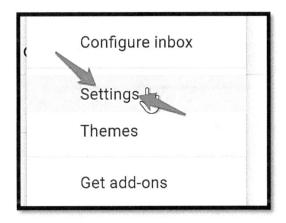

To change your preferred settings, click on any of the categories shown at the top when you are here.

Steps for Adding Contacts

The Google email system lets you save your contacts' address book. Phone numbers, birthdays, and residential addresses are all included in the address books, and your Gmail account stores these details as contacts. You should follow these steps to add a contact or contacts: first, click the Google Apps button, as indicated in the screenshot.

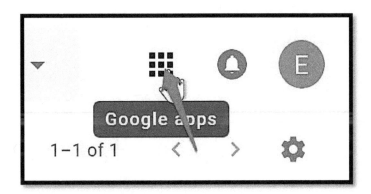

The contact button will now appear in the drop-down menu.

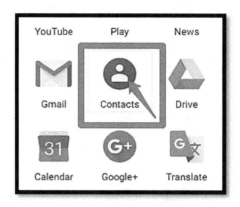

Anytime you carried out these steps successfully, the screen will display your contacts. This is when you will have to click on **add new contact** button which is located at the lower right of the display.

At this stage, add the contact information and then click onsave

Tips For Editing Contacts

You must carefully examine the Google drop-down menu before choosing Contacts in order to modify Contacts.

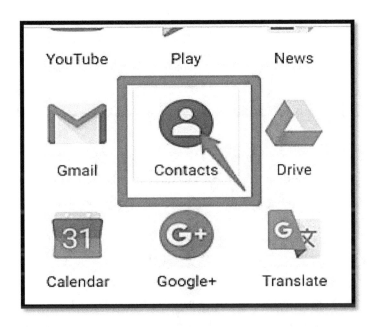

Search for the contact you want to edit and then click on Edit Contact.

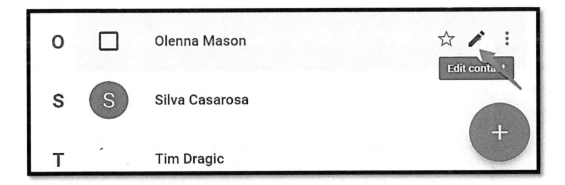

This is the time for you to make the changes you had wanted to make to the contact and then click on Save when you've finished changing your contact.

By default, Gmail keeps email addresses for you when you send emails to other users. Gmail addresses are automatically added to your contacts by the system. You must go to your contacts' address on the mail contacts in order to make the desired edits to these contacts.

Methods For Importing Email Contacts

It's possible that you have contacts stored on an email address somewhere else, but you can import contacts and messages from that email into your Gmail account using Gmail. That system is supported by most email services. The feature of importing messages and contact addresses from email accounts into Gmail is supported by Yahoo, Hotmail, and AOL. The methods below will assist you in adding your other account to your Gmail account. After you click on the symbol in the upper right corner of your website, you may choose Settings. Once you've completed this, select Accounts and then Add a mail account. From there, you may import your mail by following the instructions on the page.

About the Google Applications

Nearly everyone uses an Android phone these days, or something similar, with Google Play services, which allow you to download a wide range of apps. You can only access Amazon Apps on a computer running the latest version of Microsoft Windows 11; Google Play stores do not offer this feature. We will mostly talk about Google Apps, which let you find the apps you desire on Google Play Stores. The Google Play Store is available on most phones, allowing users to download and install apps for free or at a cost. Google's user interface has been modified. The new user interface has a few minor adjustments that set it apart from the previous version.

In the google play store: new themes

This new appearance comes after the previous UI redesign, which provided us separate tabs for games and apps. It's noteworthy to note that the previous hamburger menu, which had a three-line icon and was situated in the upper left corner of your page, was replaced by the new interface. These days, everything is found at the account switcher, which is on the upper right corner. You can access nearly anything, including the games and apps, from the upper right corner. You also get play protect, settings, and subscriptions. The number of outstanding updates is displayed on the overview tab of the new interface. It also includes storage details and an app sharing option. Ratings and review options are also included. There's a manage tab in the interface where all of your installed apps and games are listed, along with a dedicated gaming section.

Looking at the screen, you will notice that the search result has a somewhat larger app icon, as denoted by the red-colored arrow. The UI has undergone significant changes. For instance, the tabs for Updates, Installed, Library, Share, and Beta have been replaced with two new tabs called Overview and Manage. These tabs are located beneath the newly added Manage applications and device area. You also observed that the area labeled "My apps and games" had vanished.

Th Google Play Store Navigation Guide

You can locate anything in the latest Google Play Store update by following the instructions in this section if you are unable to browse the user interface. All you have to do to get back to the old hamburger menu is to tap the account switcher, which is your Google account with your profile photo, located in the upper-right corner. As soon as you click on this, a new pop-up with several components will appear.

The following are the sections:

- How to Manage Apps and Device
- The Library
- The Payments and Subscriptions
- The Play Protect
- The Notifications and offers
- The Play Pass
- The Settings
- Help Feedback

Management Guide For Games And Apps In The Google Play Store

This section contains information on installed apps, app updates, app ratings and reviews, and storage guidelines for your device. You will find sections explaining how to share an app and manage your storage alongside the option to delete undesired apps when you wish to update your apps. You only need to tap on it to see if there are any new updates or information about a new app you want to check on in order to find out whether there are updates available for your apps. If you wish to update the pending apps, you can opt to press on and select Update all. Should you choose to remove the app, first press the storage information section. Next, pick the app by tapping its checkbox. Finally, tap the top trashcan symbol. When the Uninstall option appears, tap it. View the images below for instructions on bulk uninstalling Android apps.

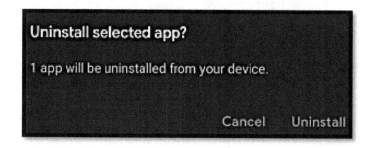

Keep in mind that you can view the specifics of the games and apps you have installed by going to the manage tabs.

About The Library

The three items in this library section are your wish list for games and apps, a link to movies and TV shows, and book apps.

The Payment and Subscription Section

All of the details regarding your subscriptions and payment options are contained in this section. You may view your Google spending history here as well. You can use this to set a monthly spending limit for apps. Additionally, there will be an option labeled "Cancel app subscription." You can just tap on it to end your app subscription if that's the case.

The Offer You Get And The Notification

You have two tabs in this section, one labeled "notifications" and the other "offers." The change regarding your Play Store account is part of this. You can find all of the exclusive offers that are accessible to you in the offer tabs or area.

The Settings Or Updates

There are four categories in this settings section: General, User controls, Family, and About. You must go to the General Settings to alter your account's preferences, notifications, and settings, as well as download preferences, auto-update programs, auto-play movies, theme settings, and other configurations. However, you can adjust the security settings for your purchases in the User control area. Under the Family area, you can adjust the Google Play Family Library Users' settings and provide parental supervision. You can use this guide to get started with the new Google Play interface. Since it's still new, this can be a little challenging and perplexing, but with these new suggestions, you can easily navigate and enjoy your new user interface. Remember that virtually everything in the new UI begins with the account switcher. The new account switcher really is the key to all the features and parts of your play store account and apps that are vital.

Modifying The Photo On Your Google Account

Everyone aspires to look well-groomed, attractive, and distinctive. There is no denying the adage that "beauty is in the eyes of the beholder." Being organized is a fantastic idea, and looking beautiful goes hand in hand with organization. Changing the photo on your Google account is a great way to stay organized and satisfy your own tastes. Image is crucial, and your taste will be satiated when you follow your instincts and maintain a positive image. It's different when you have a Google account that you may personalize whatever you choose. Google has therefore created a Google illustration tool that they have integrated into Gmail for Android. This tool allows you to generate unique profile images that are enhanced to enhance the aesthetics of your account profile. To their credit, Google upgraded Gmail in 2021 to include the capability for users of Android and iOS devices to easily update their profile photographs. Google illustrations is a new feature available on Android phones. You can select an image from a large collection of pictures or artwork using the Google illustrations. These are editable photos that allow you to add unique touches to your profile.

Selecting an illustration from Google

It is not necessary for artistic specialists to make illustrations; any Android phone or gadget can do it. Opening Gmail and searching for your profile picture or photo will be your initial steps. Usually, this is found in the upper right corner of the window. Upon selecting the profile photo, an account menu will appear. You can change this for different accounts. There is a small camera symbol on the Gmail account you just opened. Click the photo that is now shown or click the change icon that appears beneath the image. Three tabs that are labeled as drawings showing Google images and Device photos will emerge in a new menu. At this point, choose the illustrations tab. A brief action will display hundreds of illustrations for you to chose from. View the sample of the illustration tab and the several available illustrations below. You can see that the page is divided into various sections by looking at the graphics. The top is located in the explore section where specific photographs are mentioned or suggested for you to try. The following list displays many collections categorized into sports and nature. There are several subgroups within these main categories, some of which are mentioned below:

1. Technology
2. Monuments
3. Beaches and Oceans
4. Extreme Sports
5. Natural Wonders
6. Mystical Creatures.

Modifying Google Illustrations: A Guide

Once you've decided on the kind of photo you want for your profile, you'll need to tap on it to open the editor. The three customization tabs on the list are for filters, color correction, and crop and rotate. It is preferable to begin with color adjustment since it allows you to choose a specific element-based image and make a single adjustment that provides you with the color match on the specific palette you want to work with or have in mind. Every single illustration has two or more adjustable parts. Using the London Eye as an example, users can modify the surrounding natural environment, which includes grass and water. You can make use of the neighboring building's roof color. After doing this, you can experiment with filters to make changes.

The possibilities are endless when it comes to crafting the ideal profile picture. You have a variety of options for illustrations. With so many illustrations available, it will be challenging for you to decide which one to use as your profile photo. When there are so many lovely backgrounds to choose from, sometimes it comes down to personal preference or the demands of the moment. Now, tell me which illustration from the list you would pick. Fortunately, your Android phones are capable of producing the unique Google artwork required for your profile image. that is simple to obtain using the Google app, and its best feature is the ability to synchronize everything with Google Apps.

Installing the Google app on your tablets and smartphones

The Google App installation process on our tablets and smartphones has undergone numerous adjustments. Things got much more complicated with these setup and installation adjustments. It's a little more harder than it used to be to get your gadget operating if it has a Google Play store. It is a little trickier and more difficult than simply downloading an APK file and clicking a button. Many Chinese phones do not support Google Play Store in their program files, which is especially problematic if you are in China. Unlike people in America and several other parts of the world, those in China do not use Google Play. Chinese-owned Apps stores are not permitted on American phone systems, and vice versa. Installing Google Play requires a few network configuration adjustments that must be made to the play store before you can install it if you're in China. This section will teach you how to install Google Play apps on your phones and tablets by providing you with a set of instructions. Everything is dependent on how recent or ancient your tablet or phone is. Because there are so many different Android phones and tablets on the market, each with its own version, we cannot rely on a single guide to work for all of them. As a result, this guide may or may not work for you. These and a plethora of other factors could be the cause of your failure with these steps. These guidelines are a great place to start if you want to give it a try. As previously mentioned, the majority of Android phones manufactured in China do not come with Google Play Apps since China has its own regulations. One way to look at it is the potential for a manual that covers all Android/Tablet devices. I promise that this technique might make it easier for you to access the Play Store on uncertified hardware. Although it would seem so, not all devices—like Huawei flagship phones—need to perform these intricate duties, therefore not everyone can use this instruction.

It is important to remember that devices without pre-installed apps from the Google Play Store will not be able to pass Google's SafetyNet inspections. This is the reason why certain of your apps, including Google Pay, won't function correctly. Additionally, a variety of peculiar problems could arise, depending on the kind or version of Android you are using. Before you try, you'll never know what will work for you.

Potentially Useful Replacement Option

I had previously informed you that the many Android, phone, and tablet versions that are available in stores and the market will not be covered by this instruction. It is possible that after following this instruction, you will still be unable to install the Google Play Store because it is not an exhaustive guide covering all versions of phones, tablets, and devices. No manual or book can cover everything. Any book that claims to be a comprehensive reference to the massive versions of all these gadgets is lying, therefore anything more than this is a prime fraud. An all-device compatible substitute for the Google Play Store is Amazon. Like the Google Play store, they have most of the popular games. They also don't require Google services because they have a respectable selection of third-party applications. The sole drawback is that none of the Google programs, like as Gmail or Chrome, are available in their shops. The screenshot below shows you how to get apps from the Amazon App Store. The F-DROID is the name of another other app store. This mostly includes of software and games that are open-source. Although there are not many apps in this store, you might still be able to find what you're looking for. The steps to get their app from their official website are illustrated in the photographs below.

In the event that you only require a few apps, the automated updates are not very significant. Try using the APKMirror to get your apps. This is an Android app that is a play store mirror. These are safe applications that haven't been tampered with. Obtaining and approving installation from an unidentified vendor. You must first make sure that your device has the option to allow apps to be installed from unknown sources. The play store runs because of this mechanism, which lets you launch and install apps from downloaded APK files. Launching the Settings app on your phone or device is the first step. Look for the options for "unknown apps," "unknown sources," or you can search for anything in that line. If there is a search function, check for it and enter in "unknown." This is because different companies refer to options under different names. under the event that your settings app lacks a search feature, your desired choice may be found under the privacy or Apps & Notifications sections, contingent upon the specific model of Android device you are using. You should be aware that an easy-to-use switch in earlier Android versions allows access to unidentified sources. It is imperative that you confirm they are turned on. You don't need to activate the switches for each app immediately; they are displayed in the screenshot above.

Locating Information On Your Device

The file you wish to install from the Play Store will vary based on the Android OS version you have and the hardware platform of your device. The Settings app displays the operating system version together with software details unique to your device instead of the OS as a whole. To find the two pieces of information, you should utilize a third-party tool as the Fire tablet can only display the Fire OS version and not the Android version.

Getting the Play Store downloaded

Downloading the appropriate APK files for your play store is the next step in downloading the play store, which I know is vital to you. Installing the Google Account Manager, Google Services Framework, Google Play Services, and Google Play Store are the four programs you will need to do this. The account services and APIs are handled by the first three apps, but the Store itself is the final app. Obtaining the Google Account Manager ought to be your primary move. Go to the Google Account Manager website if your phone is an Android phone, or better yet, one of the more recent models. Next, press the primary "Download APK" button. You must look for the most recent app launched and select the one that is closest to your Android version if your phone is older than the Android version stated above. For example, if your Android version is 6.0.1, you need to download Google Account Manager 6.0.1. You can wait for the APK file to finish downloading instead of opening it. Do not open the APK file once it has completed downloading.

The Google Play Services download is what you need to accomplish next. This is what provides you with the majority of the Google Play Store's advanced features. You must choose the most recent releases by visiting the APKMirror page for your Google Play Services. It is imperative that you avoid using the one designated as beta. Because the APK contains two applications, each version has a single variant. Every hardware combination has a unique version of Google Play Services available as well. At this point, you need to identify the setup that works with the physical architecture of your device as well as the version of Android OS you are running. The Google Play Store is the final app you must download after downloading the APK. As everyone knows, Google releases the play store in a single version that supports every Android version and architecture. Simply visit this website and download the most recent version, which is designated as "beta." Please remember not to switch off your tablet once you have finished downloading. The Google Services Framework is the next stage. The procedure is the same as with the previous app. You need to navigate to this page on the website and choose the version type that most closely matches your Android OS version. You must use the Google Services Framework 8.10 if your Android version is 8, as I previously explained.

Installing the Google Play Store comes next, following the Google Services Framework. You must locate and open the Download/Files App on your Android device. All you need to do, if you don't have a file manager, is download and install the most recent version of File by Google, which can be found on the APKMiror. When the installation is finished, open the apps as indicated below. Next, select "Done"; kindly refrain from selecting "Open." The play store won't function if the apps are not arranged in a logical order.

Additionally, you need to confirm that you removed your SD card from your device before beginning the installation.

- com.google.gsf.**login**
- com.google.android.**gsf**
- com.google.android.**gms**
- com.android.**vending.**

Restart your device after the four apps have installed. You'll see that you can access the Play Store and log in after the boot. You will be able to download any and all apps and games after logging in.

CHAPTER TWO
ABOUT GOOGLE DOCS

A word processor included in the Google online Office Suite is called Google Docs. It is a free substitute for Word on Microsoft. You could be unaware of many of its features. You will learn about Google Docs and its features in this book. As previously mentioned, Google Docs is a word processor that runs in a browser. Google Docs allows you to create, modify, and share documents online. You can also access the documents from any computer with an internet connection. There are even iOS and Android apps for Google Docs. Google's features are what differentiate it from Microsoft Word, its main rival. As you may have seen lately, Google Docs was among the first word processors to provide online document editing. Google's cutting-edge capabilities have made it simple to collaborate on papers with others on different platforms and to edit them in real time from any web browser window. It's intriguing to you that the collaborators you share a Google document with can access and update it without even requiring a Google account. You must be aware that you may add more functionality and other things that are lacking to Google Docs by using the add-ons. Google Docs can be used in the same manner as Word documents. You must utilize Google Doc templates in order to generate new papers. Once you have shared the documents with your team, you may work together on them in real time.

The Google Doc Creation Guide

You must first go to docs.google.com and sign in with your Google Account in order to create a new Google Doc. You have the option to select a template or start from scratch when you land on the Google Docs homepage. To accomplish the same task within an already-existing Google Doc, you may also choose File > New > Documents or File > New > From template.

You can alter any part of the document, including the page orientation, using the File menu.

Ways To Save Google Documents

You don't need to remember to save your document since, as a Google Online Office Suite customer, Google saves it immediately on Google Drive, eliminating the need for a save button. When needed, you can download, email, or create a copy of your Google Docs via the File menu.

Downloading Google Docs

You should be aware that Google Drive is where they save your papers. To download a Google Doc to your computer, go to File > Download and select the file format you want.

Directions for emailing a google doc

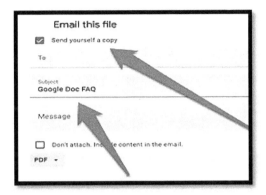

You can download a document directly from your document if your primary reason for downloading it is to email it. Simply select the file format you wish to attach and fill out the usual email information by going to File > Email > Email this File / Email colleagues. You ought to share the documents rather than sending them by email. Sharing is necessary so that everyone may work on the same version of the document and see it. This has the benefit that you won't make duplicate copies of your papers or conflicting copies of them. The recipient does not require a Google account in order to see or change the document, as I indicated in the preceding section. Click the Share button located at the upper right corner of a Google Doc form to share it with others. Recall that you have a few choices. The receivers' names or email addresses can always be entered. It's important to keep in mind that this type of procedure has a default access level, and the Editor is that default. To switch to the Viewer or Commenter pane, click the pin icon located in the right pane.

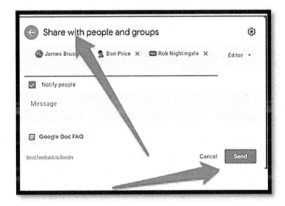

Alternatively, you may use the Get link menu or a link to share the document with groups instead than only with individuals. By default, anyone can access and share your private Google Docs. It's important for you to understand that a Google account that is part of an organization needs to be shared inside that organization. To make changes to those settings, click Change or Share. You may also give users access to the link, as well as to the Viewer, Commenter, and Editor. After finishing, select the Copy link located at the lower right corner. The link will be copied to your clipboard instantly.

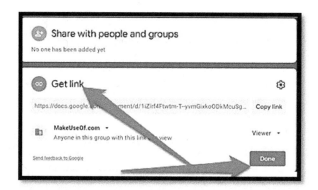

You may always utilize the create a copy trick to save yourself some tedious steps, assuming you want to share a copy of your Google Doc with other collaborators and you don't want them to change the original document.

The Docs Interface

The Toolbar, located at the top of the screen, and the document itself are included in the Docs when you are learning about the Google Doc experience. You can edit text and change the type at the same time. You can also share documents with other people.

Our Page Settings Availability

It's natural that, depending on the kind of document you want to write, you might wish to adjust the page configuration choices after creating a Google document. These options include page orientation, margins, and paper size. Clicking the Page setup link in the File menu will bring up this option. You have the ability to personalize a number of options in this page setup box.

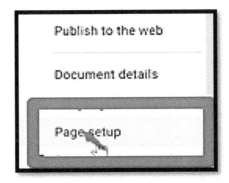

Whether your page is oriented in landscape or portrait format depends on its orientation. When you use the landscape format, your page will have a horizontal orientation. It is aligned vertically because it is in portrait format.

The spaces that appear between the document's body and the edge of the page that was taken are known as page margins.

You can alter the page's dimensions by adjusting the paper size. This is crucial and highly helpful when printing papers on paper that isn't standard size.

The page color is the color that your document's background is set to. It serves as décor. That is, if you intended to post your document online.

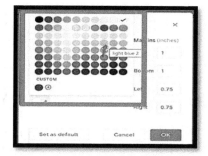

About Document creation

The most intriguing feature of Google Docs is its ability to facilitate remote online collaboration on a given project. The best thing about these Google Docs is that they safeguard your work from being lost, particularly in the event of a computer accident. When you type, Google Docs almost always saves itself automatically and allows for remote backups. Unless you are the one who erased it, the file can never be lost. You can't afford to lose it whether you're a student or a teacher working on a report, project, or term paper. Google allows you to copy and paste your work into other programs, but be aware that once a document is mistakenly erased by your computer, it cannot be recovered.

The feature that allows many users to share working documents is Google's selling point. The ability to create a Google Doc and then share it with others to edit, contribute to, or distribute the document is no longer groundbreaking; instead, it is a common practice for real-time collaboration on projects. I refer to collaborating on the same documents, typing, editing, and revising as coworkers.

Directions for generating a google document on a pc

- ❖ Visit the Gmail website, Google.com, and log in using your credentials.
- ❖ After that, select the Google App icon, which appears as a square form with nine dark grey squares on it.

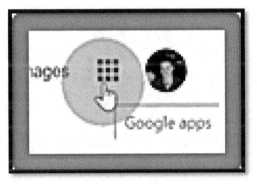

- ❖ Then you have to scroll down to the second group of apps icons that has a white stripe which is a "Doc" icon and then click on it.

The next page that comes is where you will choose the type of document you want to create and you must note that most times you want to work with it, you will first have to type in a blank page with the thick blue plus symbol.

Your Google docs will open there when you click on the "blank" document. As soon as the Google Doc has been created, you should start typing and giving it a name. This is done at the upper left corner of the pane where "Untitled Documents" will automatically appear. Once you've completed it, the next step is to share it, particularly if someone else was anticipating it.

The Document Formatting

Since Google Docs was initially released in 2006, this has been an extremely intriguing development, and Google is now the most used word processing program worldwide. Google Docs users have been praising the program for the past thirteen years because to its features, usability, privacy and sharing options, and real-time collaboration with many users. Everyone may access Google Docs for free, and corporate customers can utilize it as part of the Google Suite to get the best collaboration and cloud-based productivity tools. I must notify you that Google Docs and the G Suite are being used by over 5 million businesses to help them work more efficiently. Despite the fact that Docs is widely used, many of its users have not yet mastered all of its formatting options. Students and staff may always generate, edit, and work with a wide range of document formats, including proposals, letters, resumes, reports, and brochures, thanks to the document formatting control. Your documents will provide you the freedom you need to succeed if you can master the art of formatting Google Docs, and this means that your work will undoubtedly impress professors, clients, and employers.

Personalized footers and headers

Google enhanced its Doc with additional customization options for headers and footers. Users now have greater flexibility in formatting and customizing Word documents. Consequently, documents will appear more professional in any office or learning setting. The benefit of the new version is that it enables users to set headers and footers at the precise portions of the documents. This means that alternative headers and footers can be used on odd or even pages.

You may also be aware that before to this upgrade, users could only set one header and one footer for each document. You can test the new features by trying to add titles and page numbers to your document's headers and footers. "Different odd or even" and "Different first page" will be included in the option display. This enables you to modify the settings for the header and footer on even and odd-numbered pages.

Directions For Adding Page Numbers And Editing The Header And Footer Margins

Simply click on the appropriate header or footer, browse to the "Headers and footers" option under the "Format" tab, then pick "more options" to adjust the header and footer margins. You can input the custom margin size here. In addition to removing headers and footers entirely, you may also add section breaks. You can include a total number of pages or automated page numbers in your document. Choose "Header and page numbers" from the "insert 'tab" menu. At this stage, you can decide where the page numbers go and add a page count to the document if you want the first page to go somewhere else or to be skipped.

Apply Section Breaks To Ensure Cleaner Documents

The main purpose of section breaks is to divide and format a document into several sections. Adding it to documents is as simple as choosing "Break" from the "insert" option. This will enable you to select the "Page break," which will begin on a new page, or the "Section break," which will start on the following page and typically start with a new section. To improve the content structure, you can change the margins that separate the sections. Choose the "Page Setup" option from the "File tab" to complete this in several phases. You can now select the document portion that you would like to modify. Next, you need to create a section labeled "Ok" and specify the margins.

Manageing Organization With Document Outlines

You have to understand that the easiest technique to maintain a complex document under control and well organized is to use a document outline. You can quickly inspect the outlines of your document and make essential structural edits when it is well-organized and under control. When using a document outline, you can click on any heading in the document outline section to navigate the full document. You can avoid wasting time browsing through the lengthy document by doing this. Clicking "Show document outline," located under the display tab, will enable or disable the document outline. You'll note that Docs, drawing its outline from the headings in your text, will automatically add headings to your work. A different heading style that is available under "Normal text" on your format bar, located at the top of the browser, allows you to add. Simply choose "Remove from outline" from the document outline overview if you want to get rid of a heading.

Bookmarks: A Secure Way To Find Selection

The book function of this application is another fantastic way to arrange lengthy texts. You can instantly browse to the desired section of the paper with the use of this book function. Click "Bookmark" under the "Insert" tab after selecting the required section to utilize the bookmarking functionality. An easily recognized blue bookmark will indicate the chosen part, making it easier for you to find the key information more quickly than before.

Text And Graphic Alignment With The Ruler

One of the greatest characteristics of this enduringly popular word processor is its ability to... Users may swiftly align text, tables, pictures, and a lot more using this. The document automatically appears in the new document and contains both a horizontal and vertical ruler. By choosing the "Show ruler" option found under the "View" menu, you can work without using rulers and instantly hide them.

Quitting Formatting As Hard As It Can

It is imperative that you format your work consistently when working on a significant paper. Consistency in fonts, sizes, headings, and spacing is crucial when making a positive impression on clients, coworkers, employers, and even academics. Google Docs allows you to customize the formatting to your preference. It provides you with all the resources you require to produce fluid, understandable papers that will significantly improve the quality of your job.

Format For Painting And Clear Format

On the format taskbar is the "Paint format" option. By just clicking on the paragraphs you wish to apply the format to, you may rapidly apply your desired formatting using the paint format option. This allows you to easily alter the typefaces, text size, style, and color with a single button click. Furthermore, all you need to do to go back to default settings is to choose "Clear formatting" (Ctrl+\) if you frequently copy text from other sources and adjust formatting. You'll benefit from this from the manually formatted pasted content.

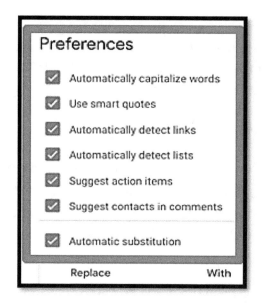

Making Personalized Replacements

There are many different default replacements available in Google Docs, and you have the right to expedite procedures. Simply go to "Preferences," which is located under the tool tab, to accomplish this. Once there, choose "Automatic Substitution," which will display a table where you can provide a custom substitution. As an illustration, you can alter your name's initials to their complete form, auto-fill email addresses, make custom abbreviations, and make sure that all frequently misspelled terms are replaced or altered to their correct spellings. Here, you may choose whether to enable or disable the "automatically detect links" and "automatically detect list" features, which will spare you from having to manually manage the format links.

Expanding the Font Set

Many different fonts are packed into Google Docs. There are numerous different typefaces, some of which include extra options for the bold features. There are many more typefaces accessible to you, but these basic fonts are quite sufficient. You must choose "more fonts" from your selection dropdown list in order to locate them. Usually, this will open a new window for you with hundreds of additional typefaces that you may add to your Google Documents. If you know exactly what you're searching for, you may either search for fonts or arrange them alphabetically or by popularity, popularity, trending, date added, or script. You can locate this under Google Docs fonts. From there, you can search, get the preview, and add the ideal font to documents right away.

Examining the abundance of templates that are at your disposal

Google Docs is incredibly significant, fascinating, and practical. It is an ideal tool for working with and creating different types of documents. It saves you hours of tedious formatting work by providing you with access to dozens of re-generated templates through its template gallery. You may access this gallery by selecting "Template gallery" under the "Start a new document" header from within your Google Docs hub. Numerous editable templates for project proposals, professional resumes, business and personal letters, meetings, minutes, notes, onboarding notes, brochures, newsletters, sales quotes, prepared essays, and much more are available in the template collection. To begin working, just choose the template you want to use, and it will be created in the new document for you. G-Suite is used by more than five million enterprises, and new versions are released on a regular basis. The quick collaboration that the G-Suite provides to employees empowers them and improves efficiency, productivity, and communication.

Document Printing And Publication

Google Docs makes publishing and printing very simple. It is recommended that you adhere to the easy measures listed below in this section. To begin, click the file to see the backstage view, where you may set up your workspace. Where to click on file number one is shown by the red arrow.Once the file has been selected, click the designer checker, which has a red arrow pointing to it.

➤ The screen you see below is what you will see after pressing the designer checker. The design checker is a tool that can assist you in finding what you want to print, and it shows what you want to print on the screen. The red arrow pointing to the outcome in the design checker window indicates the button.

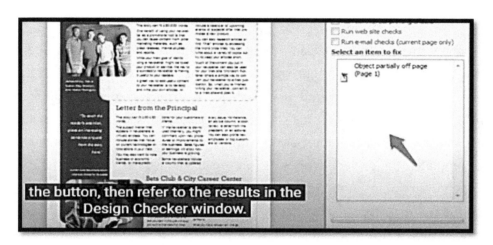

➤ On page 1, click on the slightly off-page object located at the top button on the right, as indicated by the red arrow. That is to say, something is partially suspended off the page.

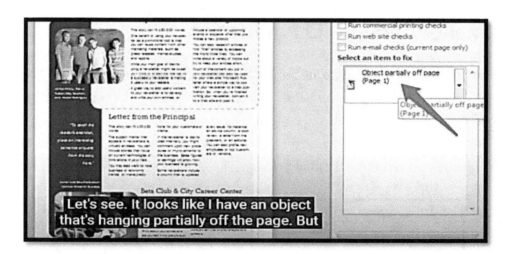

➤ It is a little too large to print, as you can see when you click on it. It refers to the shape on page 1. That's where the page size needs to be changed.

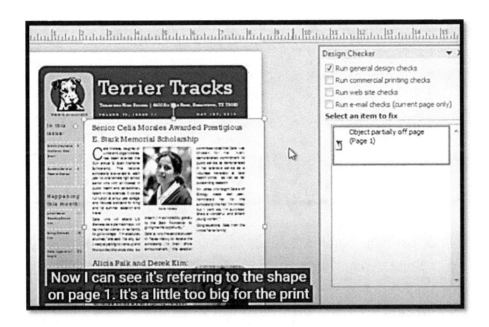

> ➤ To adjust the page's size, click the right side of the page within the page, as indicated by the red arrow. This will allow you to reduce the page's size.

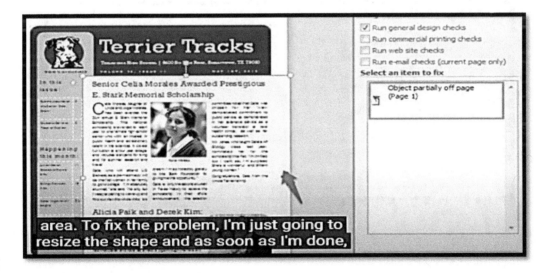

> ➤ Go back to backstage view after adjusting the page's size. If you are familiar with Publisher 2007, this task will be considerably simpler for you. Simply click the file where the red arrow indicates.

> All of the information will appear as it is on the screen below if you simply click "Print." When you're done, you'll check to see whether the print mode is missing; if not, you'll print a confirmation that everything is in the correct sequence.

> Select the copies of the print job in the next step that appears after clicking the print button, denoted by the red arrow, on the screen below.

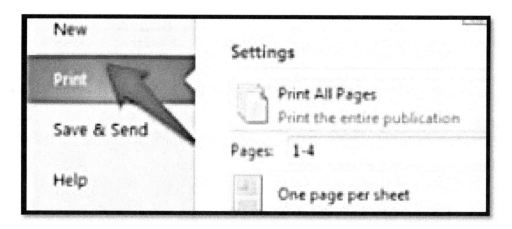

> Using the red arrow in the top left of the screen, select how many copies you wish to print.

> The settings, pages, letter, and one-sided print screen will show up. Simply select "Print one-sided." Keep in mind that you can only print on the front and back of the paper when using double-sided printing.

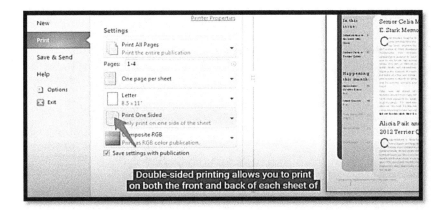

The pictures screen below is indicated by the red arrow in case you want to print on both sides, to enable the settings, click on "Print" on both sides as indicated by the red arrow

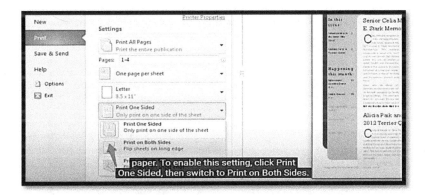

Remember if it is only on one side of the document you want to print, click on print One-Sided, if not, switch to print on both sides.

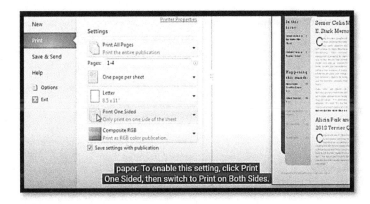

Open the menu to choose the collated as indicated on the screen below.

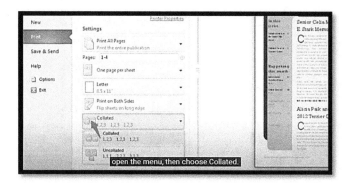

The last thing to do is to choose the colour settings for your publication. The red allow indicates the Composite R&G where click

Now, you will see different colours to choose from, let's assume you decided to choose grey as shown, when you click the colour, your print will automatically turn to grey.

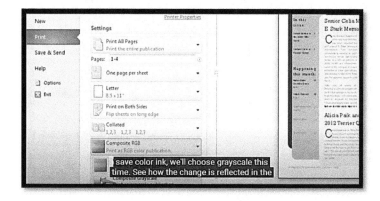

Take a look at how the page you want to print has turned to grey because you chose the colour grey. You must make sure you double-check your work before you print.

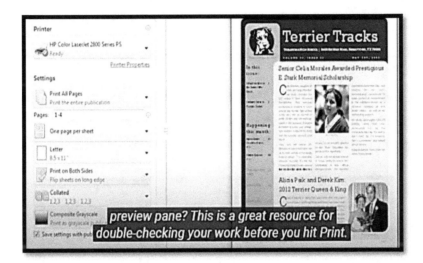

When you are happy with your settings, click on the print which is at the upper side of the left-hand corner.

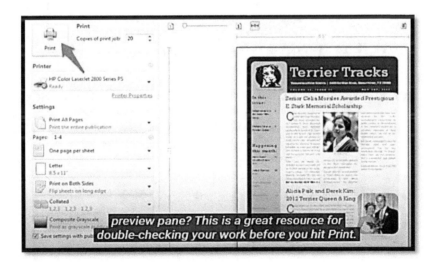

A Document's Publication

Click the file to go backstage in order to publish a document, as demonstrated below.

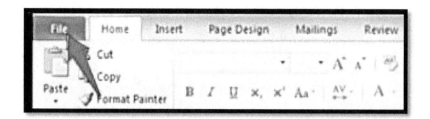

After selecting the file, select "Save & Send" from where you can publish with HTML or produce a PDF/XPS document, as shown by the illustration with the red arrow. You may now also create a PDF that you can upload to a website or attach to an email.

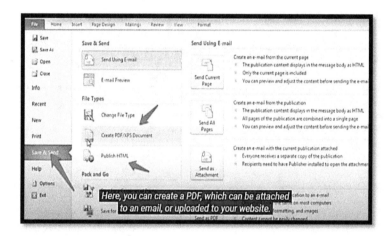

You can also publish with an HTML file which you can embed inside an email if you want.

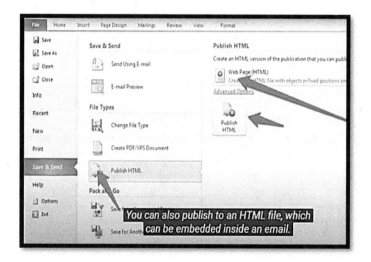

Since PDF publishing is so much better, we will utilize it in this case. Simply select the "Create PDF/XPS Document" button located on the right.

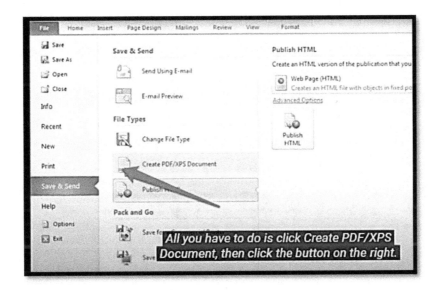

Simply click on Create PDF/XPS document and then click on the right button as shown below,

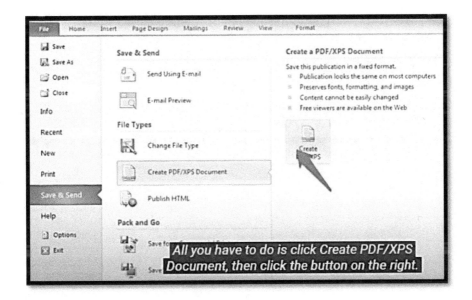

The next thing is to enter a file name and choose a location on your computer and click publish to save.

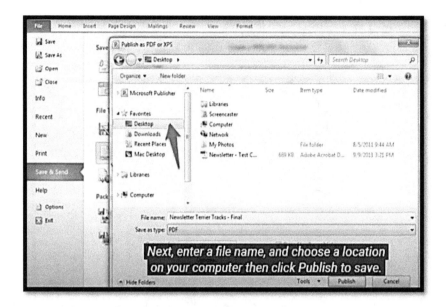

Depending on the size of your file, publishing could take up to a minute. The PDF will open in a separate window after it has been prepared. You now know how to publish content online.

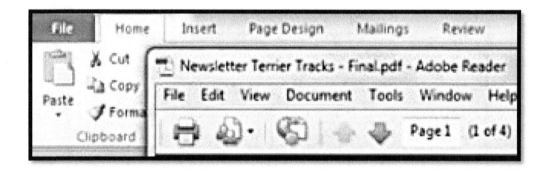

CHAPTER THREE
ABOUT GOOGLE DRIVE

You need a Google account in order to set up a Google Drive. The process of creating a Google account is simple and comes at no cost. You must submit your personal information, including your name, location, and date of birth, while creating a Google account. For the benefit of those who already have a Google Play account, let me demonstrate how to log in before we go over how to create one. Following this, we'll go over how to set up an account for those who don't already have one and are using it for the first time. That seems like the proper course of action. Google Play is available on the internet, mobile devices, and desktop computers. To access online, just type drive.google.com into your computer's internet search bar. Alternatively, you can access Google Drive by using any Google product. **Simply navigate to the waffle menu on the right on the internet, as seen below.**

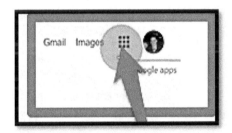

Once you've done that, the screen will display a number of alternatives for you to select, as illustrated below. To access the drive, simply click on it from the list, as the red arrow indicates.

49

On your computer, you can also install a driver. It may be configured to automatically synchronize your files and folders with Google Drive. Click the settings gear, as indicated below, with the red arrow pointing to the location where you need to click to access the backup tool. All you have to do is click on the Get Drive for Desktop link, indicated by the red arrow, in the subsequent pop-up window. After that, you must click on the download after scrolling down to the backup and sync section.

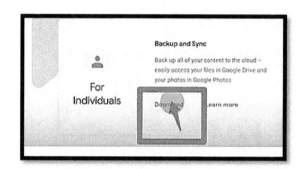

After you select "Download," a cloud backup of all of your data will be created, making it simple for you to access your Google Drive files and Google Photos images. You may use your Android phone to access Google Drive by searching for it in the app store. When you click "open," Google Drive will open right away and you will see the result for Google Drive in the third picture, as seen below.

The Starter User

You must create your Google account in the manner described in Chapter 1. Next, open your web browser and navigate to http://drive.google.com. Alternatively, you can click the drive as seen below after selecting the grid-icon in the upper right corner of any Google website, such as Gmail or the Google search.

The interface for Google Drive

You will need to learn a lot of things as you upload and create files, even though your Google Drive may be empty right now. For instance, how to use the UI to see, manage, and organize. To acclimate to the Google Drive interface, click the icon below.

Mobile Device Optimization with Google Drive

Both iOS and Android users can access this. You may use your phone to view and upload files to Google Drive by using the Google Drive mobile app. Documents, spreadsheets, and presentations can be created and edited using a separate mobile app available from Google.

Google Drive is available for use on desktop computers

If you are among those who would rather work on a desktop, you can download the Google Drive desktop application on your computer. You may operate offline with this Windows OS X program, which also makes it much easier for you to transfer your current data. Your computer will display the Google Drive folder as soon as you install it. Files moved into this folder will be uploaded to Google Drive automatically.

An Overview Of Google Drive

What gives you a location to keep your stuff is Google Drive. Google Drive is not connected to any hardware, including computers or gadgets. Despite not yet being connected to anything, it may be accessed from any location in the globe. You can use it on computers at home, on the go, or on any public computer in a library or school. Cloud storage is the name given to this kind of storage.

Google Storage's features

15 gigabytes of free storage are available. You must pay for extra storage if you need it. It has the ability to download and upload. Free desktop publishing software is included with it. You can access this by using your Google Drive account.

> - The Google Docs in Microsoft word
> - Google Sheets in Microsoft Excel
> - Google Slide in Microsoft Powerpoint.

It permits file sharing, which implies that other users of Drive can see and edit simultaneously when necessary.

The Google Drive Accessibility

All you need to do is have a Gmail account. To begin with, navigate to Google.com and click the Gmail link in the upper right corner of the screen. Using your login name and password, log into your account to proceed. Next, as previously mentioned, click on the waffle iron in the right-hand corner.

The Drive icon should be clicked as the following action.

How to Use Google Drive Without a Gmail Account

This is to let you know that any email address can be used to access a Google account. Simply visit https://accounts.google.com/signupwithoutgmail to complete the process. Next, fill up a form using the email address that you choose, such as Yahoo, Hotmail,

Comcast, etc. All of the information provided on the form must be entered. Accepting Google's terms and conditions is the final step.

The layout of the screen in the left menu

- **My Drive:** shows anything you've made or uploaded, as well as the contents of your Google Drive.
- **Shared with me:** This is the location of files that you have access to but did not create. File sharing amongst driver users allows you to view documents like spreadsheets, pictures, and PDFs. With this, you may send them without using an attachment.
- **Recent:** This displays the files you stored or viewed in the last day, week, or month, although it varies depending on how frequently you use it.
- **Starred:** This is similar to putting something in your favorites and marking it. Clicking the star icon enables you to quickly view it in the future.
- **Trash:** The files you no longer want are displayed here. It ends up in the garbage when you empty it.

The Center For The Screen Layout

This is the My Drive Toolbar, which shows the Google part that you are currently browsing. These could be recent items and pictures.

❖ **Quick Access:** The files you have recently accessed or those you use often are displayed here. The File List shows every file that is kept on Google Drive. The file list will include the following headings: (Name, Owner, Last updated, and File Size.) They are arranged in alphabetical order of storage. Clicking on the headings will always allow you to sort a certain category.

❖ **Folder icon,** you have to double click on this icon to be able to view files stored in the folder

❖ **Google docs icon**

❖ **Google sheets icon**

❖ **Google slides icon**

❖ **PDF**

❖ **Toolbar :**This is togged in between the List view and Grid view.

This turns on and off the details and activities section of the screen.

My Drive Information / Activities

Activity: Press and hold a file name or file folder once. You must be aware that the times and dates on which you or other users added, altered, or removed files are displayed in the activity part of the website.

Details: This is what offers precise details about a single, unique file.

- It shows you shared/Not shared a document.
- It shows you the type of file for instance (Doc, sheets slides, etc).
- It shows you the size.
- It shows your location.
- It shows who the owner is
- It shows you how to modify, open and create dates.
- It shows a description that adds to your description of file content.

The Updated Button

In Google Drive, new files and folders can be created. We have listed these folders below for your convenience.

- Folder: This allows you to create a new folder and also helps you to organize it.
- File Upload: This is what you can use to move multiple folders, one after the other.
- Google Doc: This is for word processing.
- Google Sheets: is for spreadsheets
- Google slide: This enables presentation in slides.
- More: Google Forms, Google Drawing, Google My Map, Google Sites

The official Google Docs, Sheets, and Slides

You have to be aware that Google uses browsers for all of its software. They are exclusively available online or through the web. Google software also utilizes the menu structure. The Office tabs and ribbon are not utilized by them. Their buttons and menus are static, never changing. Google Docs files can be modified with Word, Excel, and other programs. adds-on. This tool runs in a browser. As both of us are aware, Google offers simple access to a number of other services, including advanced chat tools, formatting tools, mail merge contacts, and more.

The Save, Change the Name, And Copy

Save: As soon as you input the first character of a new file, it is immediately saved to Google Drive. You won't have to store your file anywhere. Every modification you make is automatically stored. Check or look at the next menu; "saving" will be there, followed by "All changes saved in the drive," if you want to be sure it's saving.

Changing name:

➤ Google Drive assigns an untitled Doc, Spreadsheet, or presentation name to any file that is created there. Your file will be renamed by you to the appropriate name of your choosing.

➤ Make a direct click on the document with no title, located in the upper left corner. Next, type the name you think is appropriate. Use of punctuation, tiny and large letters are all acceptable.

Make a copy: The first thing you should do when modifying a document that you have already prepared and you need to save the original is go to File, Make a Copy. When you do so, you'll be able to save the file in a separate folder and either create a second file with a different name or keep the original file name. This functionality is identical to Microsoft Office's Save function.

About the file menu

57

- **Move to:** This method transfers a file from its original folder to a new one. Move to Trash: this action relocates the file to the trash can. To fully erase something, you must empty the Trash.
- **View the History of Revisions:** All of your files are saved with points created by Google Drive. It allows you to go back and review the files you previously edited or where you made changes, and then restore your documents without losing them.
- **Collaborators via email:** If your file is shared, you can interact with anyone who has access to view it by using the link.
- **Email attachment:** Your file will be converted to a PDF with office extension (.docx,.xlsx,.pptx, etc.) whenever you send it as an attachment.
- **Save as:** The file is immediately saved on your computer's hard drive upon download, unless you desire to save it to another format, such as Word or PDF. To save the file on Google Drive, go back to the Google Drive home screen and select New, upload file.
- **Print:** It needs to be sent to a network or local printer.

Google One's features and plans

When we discuss Google One, we are referring to its monthly membership service that provides you with more online cloud storage that you can use with Gmail, Google Photos, and Google Drive. We can store up to 15GB of files and photos on the free storage service Google Drive. In 2018, Google Storage Plan was superseded by Google One. You must now subscribe to the Google One plan if you require any additional storage on Google Drive beyond the 15GB that is provided for free. You can use the Google One app or the browser to access your Google One. Google One is not necessary nor required, however you will need it if you want more storage.

Directions For Applying For Google One

Visit the Google One page and make sure you are logged into the Google account you wish to use in order to join up. You will see that you currently have 15GB when you poke around. Additionally, it will indicate how much of the allotted 15GB of storage you have already used and how. (Google Photos, Gmail, or Drive). You are free to continue using the 15GB of free storage or to subscribe to Google One; both options are available to you. According to a Google recommendation, you may sign up for the first 100GB tier for $2 per month, giving you access to six levels. Google will verify your purchase and balance when you click on that. You can now proceed by clicking on subscription after that.

What Google One Costs

The sort of tier you have selected will determine how much Google One costs. There is no free trial period available for this, and the standard Google Drive 15GB has no costs associated with it. It's totally free. It would be beneficial for you to look at the various costs for the various levels below if you wish to choose Google One and want more than 15GB of free Google Drive space.

- 100GB: You will get it at $2 a month or pay annually at $20
- 200GB: You can get at $3 a month or per anum at $30
- 2TB: $10 a month or 100 dollars annually.
- 10TB: you can get at $100 per month.
- 20TB: Sold for $200 a month.
- 30TB; Sold for $300 a month.

The Plan for Google One Membership

100GB, AT $2 MONTHLY PLAN: You may utilize 100GB of storage on Drive, Gmail, and Photos for $2 a month, or $20 a year. Additionally, you will have access to a team of Google specialists via chat or email around-the-clock for any questions you have about technical issues or emergencies. With your Google One membership, you may share your plans with up to six family members, allowing each of them to benefit from additional capacity in their personal Google storage. It also offers free and cheap material on hotels or Google Stadia, which is an additional bonus. Redeemable through family members with whom you have communicated your plans. It automatically backs up the contacts, messages, movies, and images on your Android phone. 200GB AT $3 MONTHLY PLAN: This offers you more storage space in addition to the benefits of the 100GB plan. Additionally, members who purchase from the Google Store will receive 3% cashback. $10 PER MONTH PLAN FOR 2TB: This plan includes all the benefits of the first two, plus an extra 10% cashback on Google stores and an Android phone VPN for users. OTHER SCHEMES: You have to be a Google One member in order to access 10TB, 20TB, or 30TB, which implies you may have previously paid for the plans I originally stated. Although there is a lot of storage, it is too large for the typical individual to use.

How Google One VPN Operates

VPN connection through Google One is often available to users on 2TB or higher plans. You may get online protection with this VPN, which is integrated within the Google One app. The VPN option is located under the app's home tab, which you can scroll to. When you are on the next screen, you can swipe to turn it on. Google One allows you to book a pro Session with Google specialists to get additional information about VPNs and internet safety.

Partnering With Your Summary Family

You can add up to five groups of extra family members if you have the Google One premium membership. These five family groups are the ones with whom you can discuss your ideas. The group's access to Google Family Calendar, Family Keeps, Google Assistant, Family Link, Youtube premium plans, Google Play Family TV, and many more resources is made possible by the formation of family members. Open Google One on your browser or on the app to begin adding contacts. After that, you must add family members to your browser's home screen by going to Settings > Manage Family Settings > Manage Family Group in the app. Next, select "Invite Family Members" and press the plus symbol. Next, enter the recipient's email address, hit the send button, and your family members will receive an invitation. As soon as they approve, their profile images will appear next to yours as members. Simply click on the person's profile and choose "Remove member" to have them deleted.

How To Use Google Expert For Chat

All you need to do to obtain additional assistance with the Google one is click on the Support tab. Choose a language in which you feel most comfortable expressing yourself; their specialists are available around-the-clock. There is always an expert available to help you 24/7, whether you want to chat, email, or even fill out a form.

Client for Google Drive Desktop

The Google Drive integration makes using your PC rather simple. Go to the Google Drive Download page to begin the process of installing Google Drive on your computer. You will see a large blue button on the page that says "Download Drive for Desktop." Click the button, and your browser will ask you what you need or want to do with the file. Alternatively, it may begin downloading the file right away without prompting you. Simply save the file and open it on your PC when prompted. Once the setup file has been opened, simply follow the instructions to install Google Drive. Google will inquire about the account you wish to use. Select any of them to use for file storage. Google allows you to add more accounts if you're the kind of person who has numerous accounts. You will be able to easily identify the two virtual drives in file explorer or the finder when you do this.

After installing everything, Google will ask you to select between two options: a mirrored file and a streamed file. The mirrored file is stored locally on your computer and on the cloud, so you can work with it offline when your device is not connected to the internet. When you check the file, you will be asked to choose between the two options. If you installed Google Drive primarily to save space, you should use the streaming files, which are only stored on the cloud and can update automatically whenever you make changes locally.

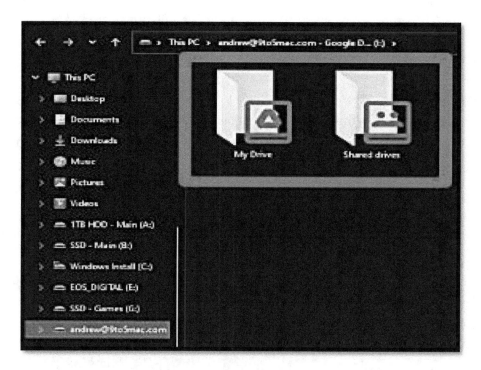

Directions For Uploading Google Photos To Your Pc From Your Drive

The alternative is to open the Google Drive configuration window and add the folder you want to backup. Drive will prompt you to choose between backing up a new folder to Google Photos or Google Drive when you add one. Organizing your images in a different location from your other documents and files will make this look more professional. Simply select the Add Folder button from the My Computer page when you're ready to upload your pictures. After you click on it, you may choose which folder on Drive, Google Photo, or both contains the photos you wish to backup. Once your decision is complete, click Done to proceed to the next page and confirm your choice. Once the process is complete, Google Photo will create a backup of the folder of your choice. Occasionally, depending on when these images were taken, you might see that the photo has been moved to the Google Photos history. If this happens, don't panic; you will eventually see it.

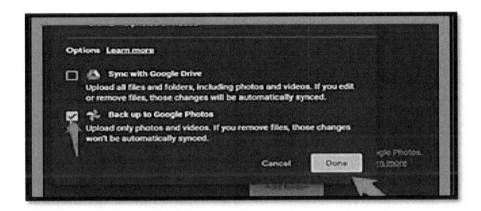

Displaying Images And Packages

You will discover how to share files and folders within Google Drive in this section. We are aware that you can transmit links to one or more of your files to members of your family or other individuals on Google Drive. Additionally, sharing is possible with a single email address or your mailing list.

How to distribute a file to a mailing list or email address

➢ Open Drive on Google.com.
➢ Select the checkbox next to the folder or file you wish to share.
➢ After that, select the share icon.

otherwise

➢ To share, click the More menu and choose it.
➢ Select "Private," "Anyone with link," or "Public on the web" as your visibility option.

Next, fill in the text box below with the email address of the individuals you like to share your file with. You can select from your contacts, establish a mailing list, or add a single individual. Selecting the appropriate access level from the drop-down menu and selecting "Can view," "Can comment," or "Can edit" next to each collaborator is required. This is depicted in the image below.

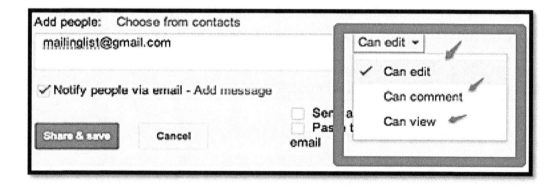

Next, select "Save" and "Share." Remember to send an email notice to everyone on your mailing list whenever you share something. To make the shared item appear in their list of documents, subscribers to your mailing list must click the link in the email message. Provide a shared file link: You can still send the link to someone else so they can get and read the file, folder, or Google doc you sent to friends, coworkers, or anyone else with the "link" or "Public."

- ➤ Visit drive.google.com.
- ➤ Select the checkbox next to the folder or file you want to share. c. Press the share icon.

Otherwise

- ➤ Select "Share" from the More menu; b. Copy the URL shown at the top of the sharing options.
- ➤ Share the link via email or chat with a different person or your mailing list.

GOOGLE DRIVE APP for smartphones and tablets

With 15GB of free cloud storage, Google Drive is a convenient software for smart or Android phones. You can access your files from any phone or tablet with an internet connection. You should have been asked to add your Google account when you first set up your Android phone because it will allow you to use Google Drive. You can configure your personal Google Drive on your tablets and smartphones by following the steps shown below.

How To Add Your Account To Android's Google Drive

The first step is to create a Gmail account on your phone, which has been covered in detail in earlier chapters. Steps 1 through 3 below must be completed after opening Google Drive and creating a Gmail account.

Step one: Open Google Drive from your home screen or app drawer

- ➤ Next, press the arrow located at the lower right corner of the screen.
- ➤ Following that, you must hit the done button in the lower-right corner of the screen.
- ➤ In the upper left corner of the screen, tap the menu button.

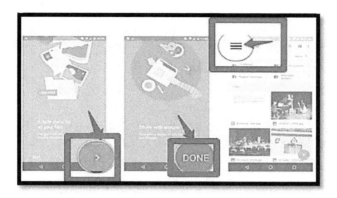

Hit the dropdown arrow that is next to the associated current account with your Google Drive. Tap the Add account. After this, you have to type the type of account you will like to use.

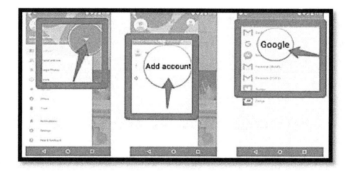

Go into a security measure that is if you have a Pin lock on your phone. After this, you have to enter your email or log-in credentials. Then tap Next, type in your password and after which you will tap on next which is at the bottom right corner.

Afterward, tap on Accept. After this then tap on the circle that is next to the payment option, tap on Continue

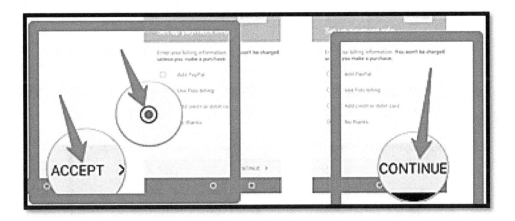

What happens now is that this account will be now added to your phone and you can use it with other Googe apps like Gmail, Docs, Sheets, and a lot more.

CHAPTER FOUR
ABOUT GOOGLE SLIDES

You can make dynamic slide presentations with Google Slides. There are a lot of slides in this presentation, and they include films, narration, animation, and much more. This section will cover the fundamentals of setting up your documents with Google Slides, including menu and shortcut toolbars, zoom settings, and theme selection.

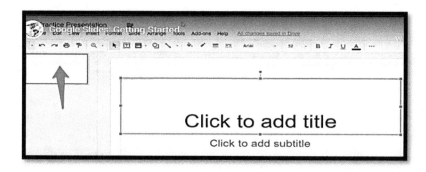

Selecting A Theme

Recall that when you make a new presentation, the Google slide will ask you to select a theme. You should be aware that the theme allows you to modify the presentation's general style, including the selection of colors, typefaces, and slide layouts. The theme you choose from the panel on the right side of the window will be used throughout the entire presentation.

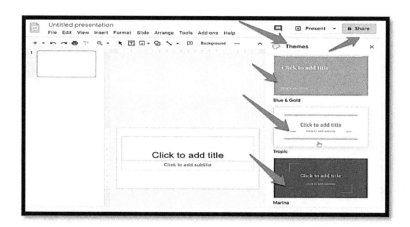

The most interesting about this is that you can choose a variety of new themes at any given time. This gives you a consistent presentation and a professional look. When you want to change your theme, open the theme panel again by clicking the theme command which is on the shortcut toolbar.

Googling Slide Science

We'll walk you through using the Google Slides environment in this part. You will discover how to zoom in and out, utilize the menu and shortcut toolbars, and more. Additionally, you will learn how to do your presentation.

The menu and shortcut tools are displayed

Google Slides has a classic menu structure with a shortcut toolbar as its interface. You need to be aware that commands on menus are arranged according to their functions. Furthermore noticeable are the buttons for their often used command on the shortcut toolbar.

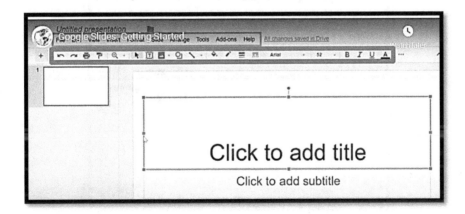

Menus That Are Show And Hidden

To make more room for you to display the slide, you can select to decrease the navigation bar. To conceal the menu bar, select the conceal menus command. All that will be left is the shortcut toolbar at the top of the window. It can be clicked to bring up the menu bar once more.

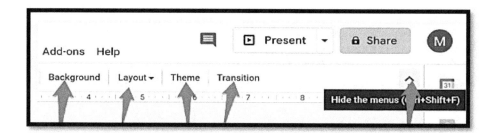

The IN-AND-OUT ZOOMING

You can zoom in and out of your presentation with the zoom shortcut. After selecting Zoom from the shortcut toolbar, you must drag the mouse pointer over the slide. The cursor will turn into a magnifying glass with a plus sign inside of it, as you can see. You can zoom in or out by using the left and right mouse clicks, respectively. To get your cursor back to normal, you have to use Escape on your keyboard. You must hover over the Zoom to reveal the ability to adjust the Zoom more precisely when you are in the view drop menu.

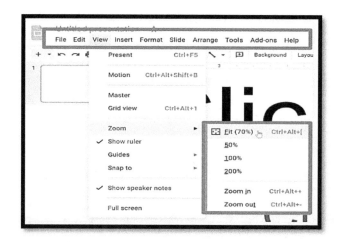

A presentation in play

Right now, everything appears stunning, which makes it interesting. All you need to do to display a presentation is select the Present option from the menu on the right. Clicking the drop-down menu for the extra presentation choice is another alternative.

Developing a Display

You will discover how to prepare a presentation, get presentation materials, and make a Google Slide presentation in this section. There are numerous instructions written in this book to assist you in making a slide show.

Firstly: set up your presentation

The most crucial stage in creating a Google Slides presentation is planning. Despite being the most crucial, the majority of businesspeople neglect or shortchange this crucial phase. Make an effort to avoid the same errors. You have to be aware that part of your preparation needs to be a thorough analysis of your presentation's objective. Additionally, be aware that you must research the audience you plan to address or try to attract. Reduce the scope of your topic and eliminate any information that is unrelated to what you are attempting to convey. Additionally, organize the information you have. You should be aware that carefully planning the order in which to create a presentation with Google Slides is crucial.

Step two: download a premium template presentation of google slide

Have you ever considered the possibility that the information you are about to share in your presentation may not be as crucial as your Google Slides presentation? You need to use a professional style while making a Google Slide presentation. You run the danger of not being heard if you don't know how to create a slide show using Google Slides. If you are not a professional designer, it makes no difference because you may still have a great slideshow design without being a professional designer. Do you know anything about Envato Elements? If not, there is an infinite collection of business-focused, expert Google Slides templates. They can help you become an expert Google Slides user.

A range of these templates are available for download, and you can also use stock images and graphics to create templates that are precisely the right size. Additionally, GraphicRiver offers a few Google slide themes and layouts. They are a pay-per-use marketplace where you may purchase premium Google slide designs.

Step three: Generate A New Presentation For Google Slide

It will be simpler for you to get started the instant you begin putting your presentation together. Google Drive must first be opened. Next, select New by clicking on it in the top left corner. Following that, select Google Slides from the drop-down menu by clicking on it. You'll see that there are now new presentations available. Keep in mind that you must upload any templates you use to your Google Drive account. The PPTX file can be dropped into your Google Drive browser. To begin working on it, double-click on it and open it in Google Slides. In other words, you have made a fresh Google Slide presentation. All that's left to do is add a theme or design to your Google Drive Slide presentation and begin adding content.

Step Four: Including Your Text

The most crucial step in producing a polished Google Slide show presentation is adding text. Your narrative will be told through your words. You can also use your words to remind people of the points you want to make in your presentation. Let's have a look at how to include text in your freshly created Google slide show. We're going to use the text box here. Keep in mind that if you are using a template, there are several text boxes on the slide. To edit the placeholder text, click on them and type over it. Typing your text is the next step that you must complete after the text box is open.

Step Five: Including Images

The slide show needs to be enhanced as soon as you begin adding text to your presentation. Using your own photos and graphic visuals is one method to accomplish this. You should be aware that include photos and graphic visuals in your presentation is not difficult. From your main menu, you must first click Insert > Images. After completing this, a drop-down menu will show up. Select the appropriate option to include your image on the slide. You have two options: use the built-in box to search the web or upload one from your PC.

Step Six: Including Entertaining Video And Audio

Insert the drop-down menu with the Audio option in the Google Slide. You can easily add an audio accompaniment to your Google slide presentation with the help of this function.

Step Seven: Selecting Automatic Or Loop Play For Your Presentation

Keep in mind that you will need to configure your Google Slide show so that it plays automatically whenever someone opens it if you need to share it online. The good news is that slide shows uploaded to Google Slides now include an auto-play feature. Select the option File > publish to the web from the menu. You will see a dialogue window that says "Publish to the Web." To have it play automatically, click the check box next to the phrase "Start slideshow as soon as the player loads."

Step eight: Modifying the appearance and atmosphere of your display

Adding or using a theme will allow you to alter the presentation's appearance and atmosphere. You can access several Master Sides and Master layouts by switching up the presentation theme.

Step nine: ways to store, export, or restore your presentation

It is not difficult to preserve your slide show while using Google Slides. This is because there is nothing for you to do. You have to be aware that your presentation is stored on the cloud. Any modifications you make are automatically saved. You need to be aware that Google Slides keeps a copy of your previous presentation. This is because you can always return to the previous version of the slide if you make changes to your presentation and later decide you want to revert to the previous version. All you need to do is click the File > Version History > view Version History menu item to accomplish this. A panel will show up on the right listing of the presentation's previous iteration.

Step ten: Presentation In Action

Your slide presentation can be presented in two different ways.

- Post it online
- Show it in real time

Use the File >publish to the web menu option to post your Google Slide online. Your website will be connected to, or you can share with your prospective audience. Click the Present button in the upper right corner of the screen to start presenting your presentation live.

Setting Up A Publication

Google Slide is a presentation tool that is a component of the free online office suite that Google provides as part of its Google Drive services. You may create and edit presentations online with the aid of this program. This saves in a file format and is tailored to your needs. Because it facilitates professional cooperation with coworkers, this Google Slide is considered user-friendly by most offices and enterprises.

Text Addition And Formatting

Launch a Google Slide presentation, then pick the specific slide to which you wish to add text. Navigate to the toolbar, select the text box option, and then click the insert button. Drag to open a text box, then type your text inside of it.

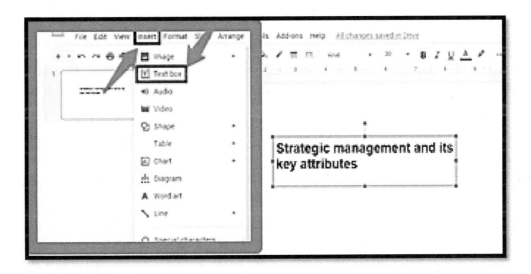

The Size And Style Of Fonts

Select the desired font type by clicking the "Font" drop-down arrow and altering the text's font style. To change the text's size, click the button next to the available font styles. You'll see that there are other font types available, such as "bold," "italic," and "underline," which you can select based on your requirements.

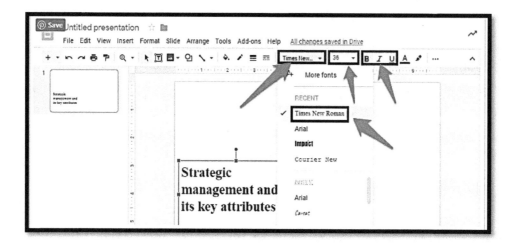

The Color Of The Font

Your text's color can be altered. To complete the task, simply select the text color choice that is situated adjacent to the font style.

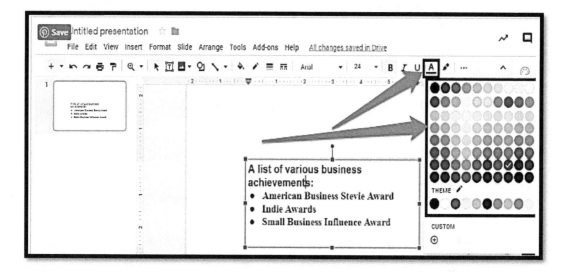

Making Text Visible

After selecting the highlight color choice, format your text to look better. Clicking the button next to the font style selection will open the panel.

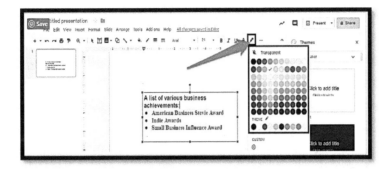

Setting a bullet point and aligning it

- Click the far right button to align or add a bullet point to your text.

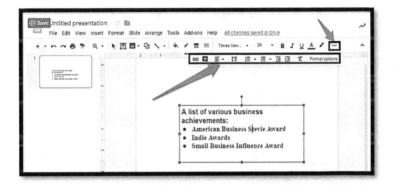

The Various Alternative Formats

You may give your text additional effects like shadows and reflections. To obtain this, select the format option, which will cause the screen panel to open. You must decide which choice best satisfies your needs.

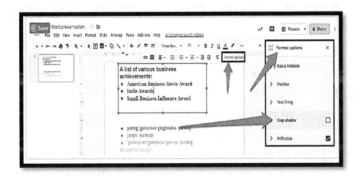

Including transitions and animation

You have to realize that slideshows don't always have to be static. I would like to let you know that you have the option of adding animations to either the slide's object or its transitions. To transition is to simply fade into the following slide or create a more dramatic effect. Recall that you may animate any object. It can be made to fade, move, or come in and out of the slide. Google Slides is excellent since it makes applying these effects simple and achievable, while also enhancing and refining your presentation. You should be aware that Google Slides allows you to manage all of your animations and transitions in one pane. You should be aware that you may set up the transition and all of the animation for the slide you are currently on in the Motion pane.

You must know that transition and animation are best used in moderation. You also know that adding too much of these can change or affect your presentation in that it will look a little silly and can also distract your audience. You have to consider using a more subtle transition and animation. You can decide not to use them too. When you want to add a transition, you have to select the desired slide and click on the Transition command on the toolbar.

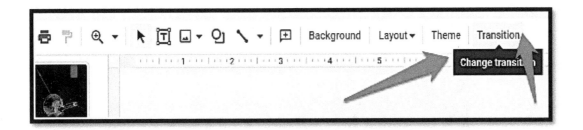

You will notice that the Motion page will appear underneath the slide transition, then you should open the drop-down menu and then select a transition.

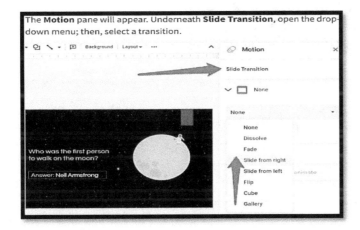

You will notice that the transition will be applied to the current slide. This also means that you can adjust the speed of the transition or you can apply the same transition to all sides.

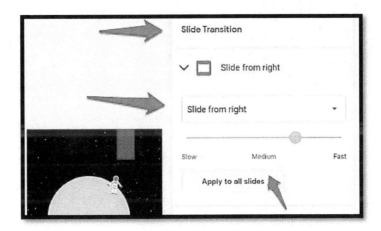

To add an animation: you have to right-click your desired object and then select Animate.

You will notice the appearance of the Motion pane. You will also notice that underneath Object Animations, a default animation will be added to your selected object and the display that is in the pane.

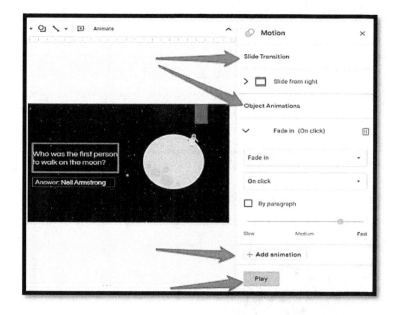

Open the drop-down menu and then make a selection of your desired animation.

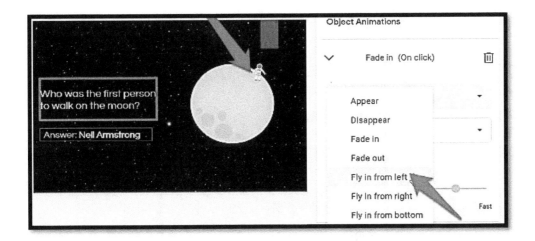

Note that if the motion pane is already opened and you still want to add more animations, you can select an object and click on add animation. You can also add a lot of animation to one object.

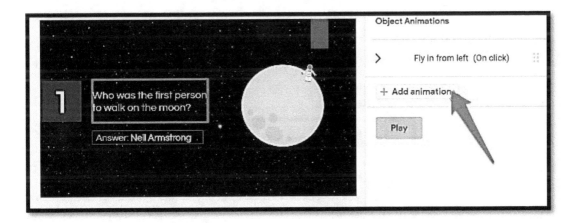

The options for animation

During a slide show, clicking with the mouse triggers the default effect. Assuming you have a multiplier effect, you will need to click multiple times to initiate each effect separately. You can then have an effect that automatically plays with or after the previous effect if you modify the start choice for each effect.

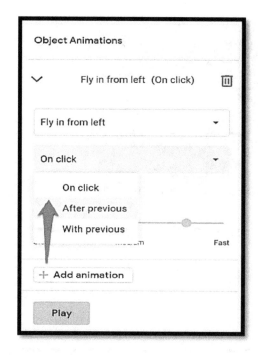

The By Paragraph check box will be shown if you observe that the object is a text box or placeholder. This establishes whether the animation is applied to the text box as a whole or animates each paragraph separately.

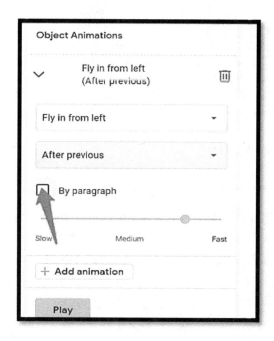

Note that you can adjust the speed of the animation by dragging the animation speed slider.

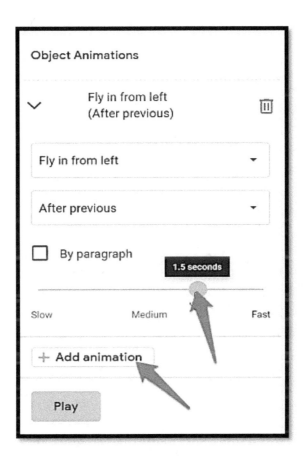

The Presentation Printing

You will discover how to print your presentation in this part. Kindly adhere to the instructions listed below.

- Start your Google Slide show.
- Press the file icon. As soon as you do that, a new window with a preview of your presentation and a setting for printing will emerge.
- To choose the printer, click the arrow to the right of the tab's destination. It is important for you to understand that in the event that a printer is not shown on the menu, you will need to add it manually through your device and set it up.

To accomplish this, take these actions:

- Navigate to Start - Configuration - Devices - Printers and scanners in Windows 10.
- Navigate to the Hardware and Sound control panel in Windows 7 or Windows 8.-
- **Add Printer:** Next, add a Bluetooth, wifi, or network printer.
- If, after completing this configuration process, the printer is still not shown, you need to verify if your computer is connected to the printer wirelessly or via a cable. To confirm your capabilities and the connection path, you must refer to the printer instructions.
- Select the Print option located at the window's bottom.

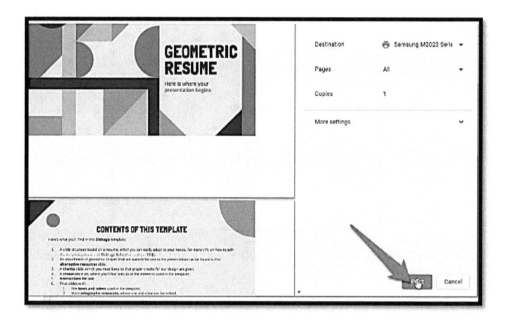

Choose The Slide You Want To Print

- Slideshow on Google Slides should open.
- To print the file, click it.
- Once you've completed that, select the pages by using the right arrow if you wish to print the entire presentation or just a portion of it. To print all of the pages, select Pages - All; to print just specific slides, select Pages - Custom.

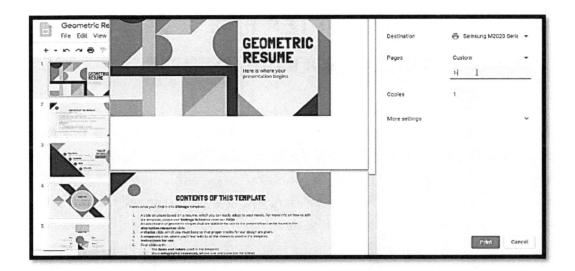

- Finally, click on the print button

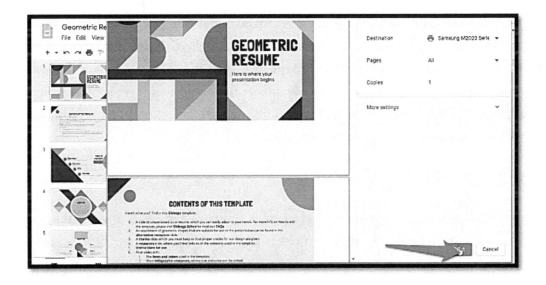

CHAPTER FIVE
ABOUT GOOGLE SHEETS

An online tool called Google Sheets enables users to create, edit, and alter spreadsheets while also sharing data instantly with others via the internet. We are aware that Google products come with standard functionalities for spreadsheets. The capabilities of the spreadsheets allow us to add, remove, and sort rows and columns. In contrast to spreadsheet tools, Google Sheets allows users who are geographically separated from one another to work together on a spreadsheet while also chatting with one another via an integrated messaging app. Spreadsheets from computers and mobile devices can be uploaded to Google Sheets. The ability to view other users' modifications while they are being made and to automatically save changes make this application excellent. The Google Doc Editors Suite, a free web program, includes the Google sheets. Google Docs, Google Slides, Google Drawing, Google Forms, Google Sites, and Google Keep are all part of the Suite. Spreadsheet cooperation occurs globally through the usage of Google Sheets. Multiple users are supported, and they can edit their Google Sheets document in real-time and at any moment. The Google Sheets online spreadsheet tool organizes and analyzes data effectively while facilitating the creation, editing, and formatting of spreadsheets online with great simplicity.

Applying Google Sheets

You may find it interesting to learn that users may utilize their iOS or Android-powered mobile devices to create and modify spreadsheets online as well as the Google Sheets online web application. You must have a working email address in order to use a Google sheet.

Users of Google sheets can perform the following:

- Spreadsheet editing and formatting: An item for a spreadsheet can be added. With Google Sheets, you may also modify, format, and apply to functions and formulas.

- Analyzing: Spreadsheet data can be visualized in conversations, graphs, and tables by using Google Sheets.
- c. Sharing: Google Sheets users are able to instantly share documents and folders.
- Downloading and Printing. Google Sheets files can be opened and imported by users into other document formats, such as Word, PowerPoint, Adobe PDF, Microsoft Excel, and PNG, or portable network graphics.

Feature-rich Google Sheets

The fundamental functionalities of Google Sheets that we utilize on a daily basis are spreadsheet editing and formatting. The processes and functions for data entry, data summary, text translation, data import, data validation, and data protection are all included in the spreadsheet formatting and editing. In order to create or restore text with unprintable characters eliminated, cleaning is also required. In order to eliminate spaces that could be leading, trailing, or repeated in the text, trimming is also necessary. Additionally, it entails heatmaps, customs conditions, date, numerical or alphabetical arrangement, and data filtering.

This employs colors to illustrate the density of data points in the table as well as other fundamental and sophisticated formulas.

- **Data Visualization:** This allows you to create graphs from spreadsheet data. Additionally, you can create other diagrams, including charts, and post them to websites.
- **The characteristics based on machine learning:** The function creates pivot tables, facilitates discussions, and responds to queries regarding the data using machine learning. You may receive an auto-update from this depending on the data choices.
- **Offline editing:** The sheet can be used offline without an internet connection. It can be edited offline, and modifications can be done right away when an internet connection is available. A number of file types, including Excel (XLS), Apache Open Office, PDF, Text, HTML, and comma-separated values, are compatible with Google Sheets.

- **The Google Product Integration:** Other services such as Drawing, Finance, Form, and Translate can be combined with these Google sheets. Several keyboard shortcut shares and Microsoft files are among the others.
- **The Collaboration Features:** Users can work together on a single document, exchange emails about other spreadsheets that are shared, provide comments for other users, and see their version history.
- **Security:** Users may request authorization to alter, download, copy, or print content for security-related reasons. This is for specialized cooperation via persons, groups, or domain access that is secured.

The interface of the sheet

You may perform numerous tasks using the Google Sheet, including organizing, editing, and using spreadsheets to analyze various sorts of data. This section explains how to access the Google Sheets interface and the various ways you can use the spreadsheet. Additionally, you will master the fundamentals of working with cells and cell content. This covers the methods of choosing cells, adding content, and then copying and pasting cells.

Concerning Google Sheet

As we learned in the last chapter, Google Sheet is a web-based spreadsheet program that functions similarly to Microsoft Excel in terms of storing and organizing various kinds of data. Although Google Sheets lacks some of Excel's more sophisticated features, creating and editing spreadsheets of any complexity is a simple process. You might be shocked to learn that a lot of individuals use spreadsheets for routine chores, even though you might assume that they are only used by particular people to analyze and tabulate their complex statistics and data. Whatever you can think of, there is a Google sheet available for your use and purpose, whether you are starting a budget, designing a garden, or making an invoice.

Guide For Making A Google Sheet

Click on New while on Google Drive, then choose Google Sheets from the drop-down box.

You will notice that the spreadsheet will appear in a new browser tab.

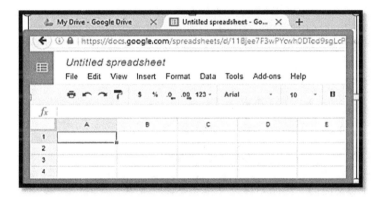

To locate and name the spreadsheet, you have to select the untitled spreadsheet which is at the top of the page. You will then press Enter on the keyboard.

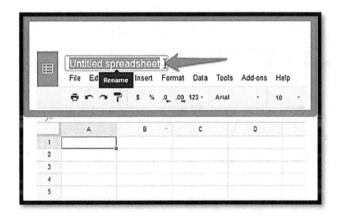

Then proceed to rename your spreadsheet.

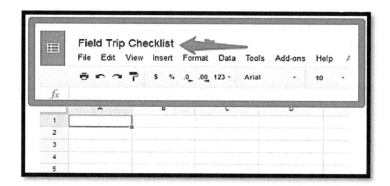

If you need to view or edit your spreadsheet again, this can be accessed from your Google Drive, where it is saved automatically.

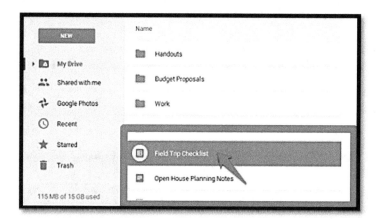

If you observe closely, you will notice that there is no save button, this is because Google Drive uses an autosave, which automatically saves your file.

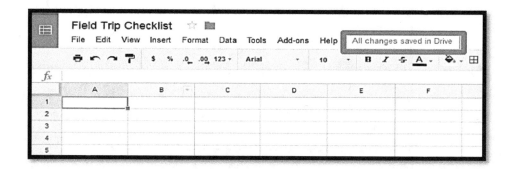

Check out the google sheet interface

The essentials of a cell

We are aware that each spreadsheet consists of thousands of cells, which are rectangular-shaped elements. A cell is defined as the point where a row and a column intersect. As you can see, columns are denoted by numbers (1, 2, 3, etc.).

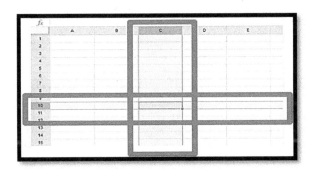

Each cell has its name or a cell address and this is based on its column and row. The example is shown above where you will see the selected intercept column C and Row 10, with this, the cell address becomes C10. You should note that the cell column and the Row headings will become darker when the cell is selected. You know that you can select multiple cells at the same time. A group of cells is defined or known as cell range. Instead of a single cell address, you will refer to them as a cell range using the cell address of the first and the last cells all in range but separated by a colon. For example, a cell range that has cells A1, A2, A3, A4, and then A5 should be written like this A1:A5. The image below shows the two different cell range was selected.

Cell range A2:A8

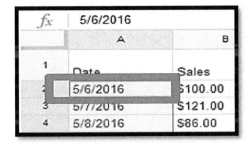

Cell range A2:B2

fx	5/6/2016	
	A	B
1	Date	Sales
2	5/6/2016	$100.00
3	5/7/2016	$121.00
4	5/8/2016	$86.00

The process of comprehending cell content

Data that is entered into a spreadsheet is kept in a cell. Recognize that different kinds of contents may be present in each cell. Text, formatting, formulae, and functions are all included in this.

- **Text:** Text is stored in cells and can take the form of letters, numbers, or dates.

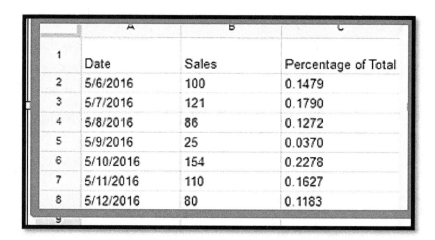

	A	B	C
1	Date	Sales	Percentage of Total
2	5/6/2016	100	0.1479
3	5/7/2016	121	0.1790
4	5/8/2016	86	0.1272
5	5/9/2016	25	0.0370
6	5/10/2016	154	0.2278
7	5/11/2016	110	0.1627
8	5/12/2016	80	0.1183
9			

- **Formatting attributes:** You will notice that cells have or contains formatting attributes that change the way letter, numbers, and dates are shown or displayed. An example of this can be when percentages appear as 0.15 or 15%. Another thing is that you can change the cells background colour as shown in the example below.

Date	Sales	Percentage of Total
May 6	$100.00	14.79%
May 7	$121.00	17.90%
May 8	$86.00	12.72%
May 9	$25.00	3.70%
May 10	$154.00	22.78%
May 11	$110.00	16.27%
May 12	$80.00	11.83%

Utilizing Functions and formulae

Cells have functions and formulae that are utilized to compute cell values. As shown in B2:B8, the example below shows how SUM(B2:B8) adds or puts the value of each cell in the range, resulting in the total in cell B9.

The Cells Selection

You must first select the cell in order to enter or modify its content.

- Click on the chosen cell first.
- A blue box will start to appear around the cell that you have chosen.

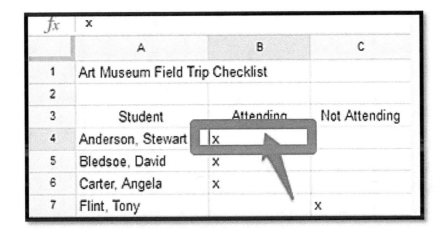

Choosing A Cell Ranging

Sometimes you'll want to choose a wider range of cells, or what we refer to as a cell group. Until every cell you are choosing is highlighted, you will click and drag the mouse. After then, let go of the mouse to choose the required cell range.

	A	B	C
1	Art Museum Field Trip Checklist		
2			
3	Student	Attending	Not Attending
4	Anderson, Stewart	x	
5	Bledsoe, David	x	
6	Carter, Angela	x	
7	Flint, Tony		x
8	Jimenez, Alfonso	x	
9	Jones, Drew	x	
10	Martin, Billy		x

A Cell's Content Insertion

- Pick the preferred cell.

fx			
	A	B	C
1	Art Museum Field Trip Checklist		
2			
3	Student	Attending	Not Attending
4	Anderson, Stewart	x	
5	Bledsoe, David	x	
6	Carter, Angela	x	
7	Flint, Tony		x
8	Jimenez, Alfonso	x	
9	Jones, Drew	x	
10	Martin, Billy		x
11	Quince, Tim		x
12	Polanski, Lisa		x
13	Olsen, Stephanie		
14	Stephenson, Anneke		

Type the content into the selected cell and the next thing to do is to press Enter. All the content will appear in the cell and the formula bar. You can also put the content into it and then edit the content into the formula bar.

fx	x		
	A	B	C
1	Art Museum Field Trip Checklist		
2			
3	Student	Attending	Not Attending
4	Anderson, Stewart	x	
5	Bledsoe, David	x	
6	Carter, Angela	x	
7	Flint, Tony		x
8	Jimenez, Alfonso	x	
9	Jones, Drew	x	
10	Martin, Billy		x
11	Quince, Tim		x
12	Polanski, Lisa		x
13	Olsen, Stephanie	x	
14	Stephenson, Anneke		

Erasing Cell Data

Choose the cell you wish to remove, then hit the delete or blank space keys on your keyboard to remove the contents of the cell.

	A	B	C
1	Art Museum Field Trip Checklist		
2			
3	Student	Attending	Not Attending
4	Anderson, Stewart	x	
5	Bledsoe, David	x	
6	Carter, Angela	x	
7	Flint, Tony		x
8	Jimenez, Alfonso	x	
9	Jones, Drew	x	
10	Martin, Billy		x
11	Quince, Tim		x
12	Polanski, Lisa		x
13	Olsen, Stephanie		
14	Stephenson, Anneke		

Cell Copying And Pasting

Copying content from within your spreadsheet is significantly simpler, and you may paste the content to the other cell. After you've chosen the cell you wish to copy, use the keyboard shortcuts Ctrl+C (Windows) or Command + C (Mac) to make the copy.

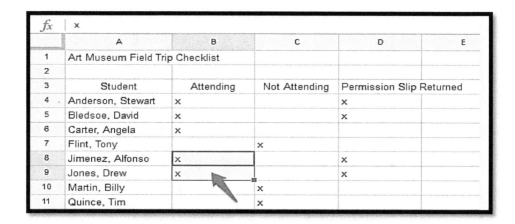

Choose the cell exactly where you want to paste the cell. You will notice that the copied cells will now have a box around them.

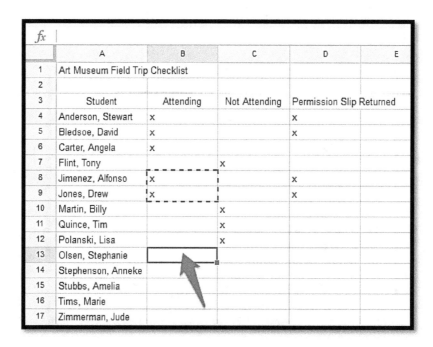

Press Ctrl+V(Windows) or the Command +V (Mac). This you have to do on your keyboard to be able to paste the cells.

	A	B	C	D	E
1	Art Museum Field Trip Checklist				
2					
3	Student	Attending	Not Attending	Permission Slip Returned	
4	Anderson, Stewart	x		x	
5	Bledsoe, David	x		x	
6	Carter, Angela	x			
7	Flint, Tony		x		
8	Jimenez, Alfonso	x		x	
9	Jones, Drew	x		x	
10	Martin, Billy		x		
11	Quince, Tim		x		
12	Polanski, Lisa		x		
13	Olsen, Stephanie	x			
14	Stephenson, Anneke	x			
15	Stubbs, Amelia				

Cells Cutting And Pasting

Cutting and pasting allows content to be moved between cells, whereas copying and pasting creates duplicates of cell content. It is necessary for you to choose which cells to clip.

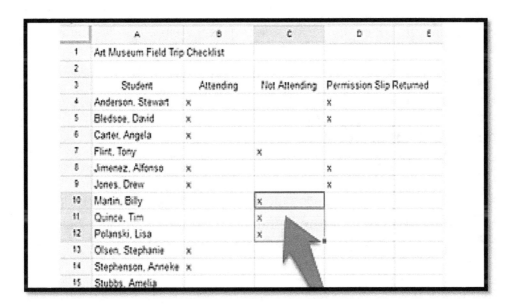

Press the Ctr+X(Window) or press Command +X (Mac). You have to do this on your keyboard to be able to cut the cells. Note that the content will remain in its original location until when the cells are pasted. You have to make a selection of the cell or the cells where you want to paste the cells.

	A	B	C	D	E
1	Art Museum Field Trip Checklist				
2					
3	Student	Attending	Not Attending	Permission Slip Returned	
4	Anderson, Stewart	x		x	
5	Bledsoe, David	x		x	
6	Carter, Angela	x			
7	Flint, Tony		x		
8	Jimenez, Alfonso	x		x	
9	Jones, Drew	x		x	
10	Martin, Billy		x		
11	Quince, Tim		x		
12	Polanski, Lisa		x		
13	Olsen, Stephanie	x			

After that, in order to paste the cells, you must hit the keyboard shortcut Ctrl+V (Windows) or Command +V (Mac). There are situations when you might want to copy and paste just specific cell contents. You must utilize the Paste Special option if this is the case. To proceed, simply select the Edit option from the toolbar menu. After completing that, select your desired paste option from the drop-down menu by moving the mouse pointer over the Paste Special.

As you drag and let go of cells

You can transfer the contents of cells by dragging and dropping them, which is an alternative to cutting and pasting. One must choose a cell. After completing that, move the mouse pointer over one of the exterior edges of the displayed area beneath the blue box. As seen here, a red arrow indicates this.

fx	x				
	A	**B**	**C**	**D**	**E**
1	Art Museum Field Trip Checklist				
2					
3	Student	Attending	Not Attending	Permission Slip Returned	
4	Anderson, Stewart	x		x	
5	Bledsoe, David	x		x	
6	Carter, Angela	x			
7	Flint, Tony		x		
8	Jimenez, Alfonso	x		x	
9	Jones, Drew	x		x	
10	Martin, Billy	x			
11	Quince, Tim	x			
12	Polanski, Lisa	x			

After that, the next thing to do is to click and drag the cell to its preferred location.

	A	**B**	**C**	**D**	**E**
1	Art Museum Field Trip Checklist				
2					
3	Student	Attending	Not Attending	Permission Slip Returned	
4	Anderson, Stewart	x		x	
5	Bledsoe, David	x		x	
6	Carter, Angela	x			
7	Flint, Tony		x		
8	Jimenez, Alfonso	x		x	
9	Jones, Drew	x		x	

Once everything is finished, let go of the mouse to drop the cell.

How To Use The Fill Handle

You might occasionally need to duplicate the contents of one spreadsheet cell to multiple other cells. You could choose to duplicate the text and insert it into every cell. Since it takes a while to copy and paste material into each cell, you can swiftly copy and paste from one cell to another in the same row or column by using the filled hand. Choose the cell that you wish to use or work on. At the bottom right corner of the cell, there will be a small square that is called the fill handle. After completing that, you must move the mouse pointer over the fill handle. The pointer will turn into a black cross, as you can see.

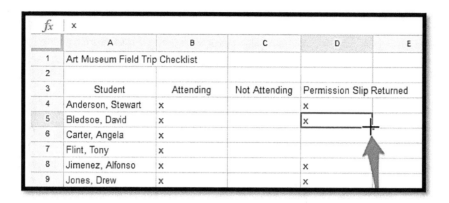

After that, click and drag the fill handle over the cell you want to fill. There will be an appearance of a dotted black line around the cell that will be filled.

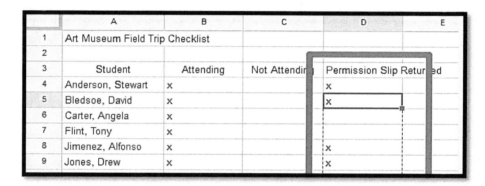

Release the mouse to fill the selected cells.

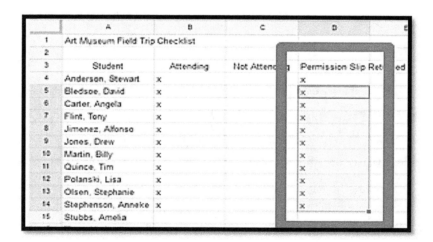

Appropriate Ways To Continue A Series With The Fill Hand

The filled hand can be used to carry out more series. Keep in mind that the filled hand will predict the next item in the series whenever the information in a row or column is arranged in sequential order, such as the numerals (1, 2, 3, or you can say days, like Monday, Tuesday, Wednesday). The example below demonstrates how a number of dates in the column were extended using the fill handle.

Specific menu sheets

This part will be included in the menu tailored to each page. It is important to remember that not all programmers and end users are aware of this, therefore forcing them into a programming environment in order to enable them to run functions makes sense. For this reason, developers of software applications create a menu that is easy to navigate and offers a wide range of options for end users to select from. We will begin by studying the useful feature that was added to the custom menu as an option.

Google Spreadsheets' Custom Menu

Obtaining the current spreadsheet is necessary, after which you must define the menu item and link each function that needs to be executed. To the active spreadsheet, add the custom menu. Could you please look at the code that would accomplish that?

```
function onOpen() {
  var ss = SpreadsheetApp.getActiveSpreadsheet(),
    options = [
      {name:"Say Hi", functionName:"sayHello"},
      {name:"Say Goodbye", functionName:"sayGoodbye"}
    ];
  ss.addMenu("Email", options);
}

function sayHello() {
  Browser.msgBox("Hello!");
}

function sayGoodbye() {
  Browser.msgBox("Goodbye!");
}
```

I took the current spreadsheet and put it in the ss variable in this code. Next, I defined the options variable. The array of items in this option each have a name and a function name. You'll see that the text you wish to show in the menu selection is the name. Moreover, you'll see that the function name corresponds to the name of the function that will execute as soon as the user chooses the option. I updated the spreadsheet with a menu. This is accomplished by passing it in the option meaning is now defined and providing it the name we want to appear as the menu name.

Step one

We will verify that the function onOpen is selected at this point by running the code. Next, we must click "Run," which appears to be a play button.

Step two

The script will ask for your permission to run. When you run a script for the first time, this will occur. Additionally, the system will inquire as to whether you added any more calls to Google App Script APIs. After that, you'll select "continue," and then "accept." After you click "accept," your spreadsheet will reopen. At that point, a fresh, customizable menu with options will appear.

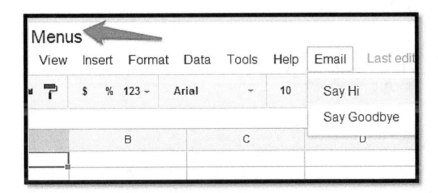

Google Document's Custom Menus

I have to assume that the coding for custom menus in Google docs differs from that of the spreadsheet.

Step one: Go to Tools > Script Editor from the menu. After that, Google will ask you what kind of script project you would like to start. Next, give your project a name by selecting a name that is blank.

Step two: You'll see that a function named myFunction() has already been developed for you. After that, we'll rename it open().

Why were you calling it onOpen, I wonder? As previously said, the Google App Script will recognize it as a unique occurrence. We should be able to write our code inside the onOpen event because the end-user needs the custom menu to be accessible as soon as they open a page.

Step three: The following three actions are what we must take:

- The document user interface must be obtained. Next, a custom menu must be created and given a name that will be displayed as the menu name.
- Include the menu item and link each function to how it ought to operate.
- The document user interface needs to have a custom menu added. That's exactly what the code that's written below will do.

```
function onOpen() {
  var menu = DocumentApp.getUi().createMenu('Email');
  menu.addItem('Say Hello', 'sayHello');
  menu.addItem('Say Goodbye', 'sayGoodbye');
  menu.addToUi();
}

function sayHello() {
  // Do stuff here...
}

function sayGoodbye() {
  // Do stuff here...
}
```

We started with the document user interface, made a custom menu, gave it a name, and put it in the menu variable. Subsequently, we included a menu choice and supplied it with a name and function name. The text you want to display in the menu option is still the name. When the end user finally chooses the option, the function name is the name of the function that will be executed. Next, we'll update the document user interface with the menu.

Step four

Now is the moment to execute the code and confirm that the function has the onOpen option chosen. Press the Run button. Run has the appearance of a play button.

Step five: The system will request your permission to execute the script. When you run a script for the first time, this will occur. If you included any new calls to the Google Script APIs, it will inquire. After that, you must click Continue and then Accept before returning to your document. Your newly customized menu with options should be visible.

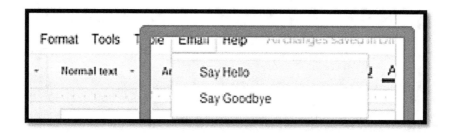

Spreadsheet Formatting

Spreadsheets that have a lot of information added to them can occasionally become hard to look and comprehend because of the information being grouped together. The spreadsheet becomes much easier to read and examine when you format it because you can alter its appearance and feel. This part will teach you how to change the text in your cells in terms of size, style, and color.

Formatting Cells

You have to realize that the spreadsheet's very cell is formatted with the identical default values. You can simply alter the formatting as you start building the spreadsheet to make it much easier to look, read, and comprehend. In this example, we will plan and arrange a garden plot using a spreadsheet.

A Change In Font Size

It is much easier to read when the font size is changed because it can draw attention to the key cells. To help us distinguish the header cells in this example from those in the other spreadsheet, we shall enlarge them. It is necessary for you to choose the cells or the desired cell to edit.

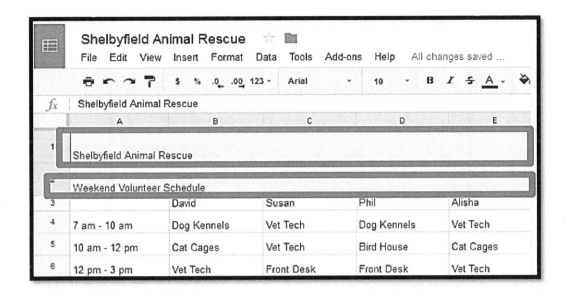

Find and then select the Font Size button that is in the toolbar after which you will choose your desired Font Size from your drop-down menu. In the example, we selected Font Size 14 as shown in the picture below,

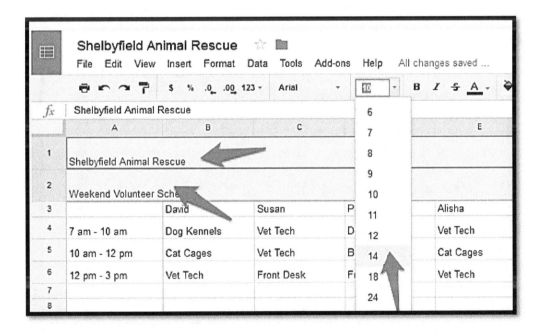

You will notice that the text will change to the new Font Size 14.

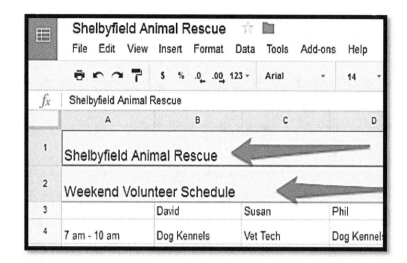

Modifying The Font

It will be easier to keep specific sections of your spreadsheet apart from the rest of your data when you alter the font, such as the header. It is necessary for you to choose the cells or the desired cell to edit. Find and pick the Format option from the Toolbar menu. Select a new font from the drop-down menu by moving the mouse pointer over the font. In the following scenario, Georgia was chosen.

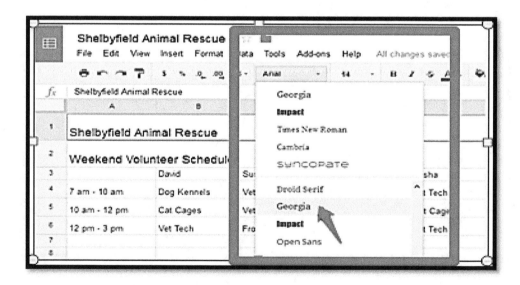

You will notice that the text will change to the new Font.

Editing The Color Of The Text

You must choose the cell or cells that you wish to edit. You next need to find and pick the Text color button from the Toolbar after completing this.

You will notice a drop-down of different Text colours appearing. You will then select the type of colour you want to use, in this example we selected red.

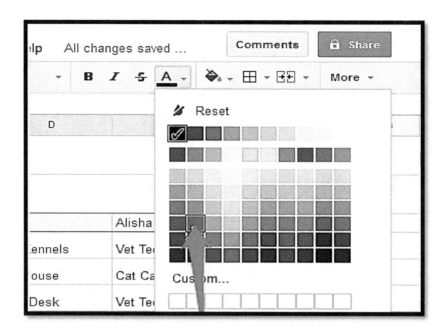

You will notice that the text will change to the new colour red.

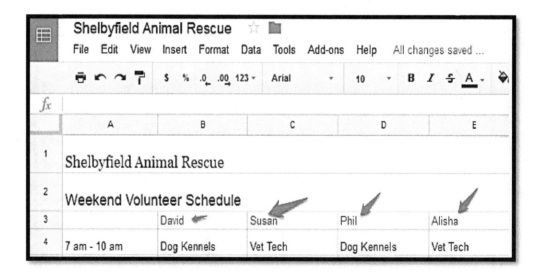

The Text Boldening

Choose the text you wish to edit, then click the bold text button or use the keyboard shortcuts Ctrl+B (Windows) or Command + B (Mac).

You will notice that the text will change to Bold.

Press Ctrl +I (Widows) or the Command +I (Mac) on your keyboard to be able to add the italics, or press Ctrl+U(Windows) or Command +U (Mac) to add the underline as shown below,

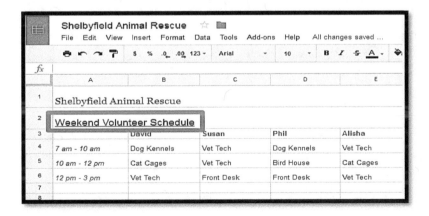

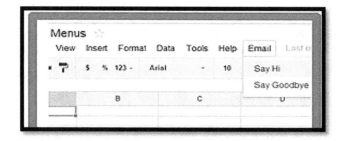

- **Go to Tools > Script Editor in Step one:** The project for which you wish to write the script will prompt you to type it into Google. Give your project a name after selecting a blank project.
- **Step two:** You will see that a function named my function() has already been created for you. It can be renamed as onOpen().

```
function onOpen() {

}
```

I called it onOpen(), but why? The Google app will be able to recognize it as a unique event. You type some things, and it doesn't pick them up. Code should be developed to make your customers available within the onOpen event if you want them to be available as soon as an end-user opens a spreadsheet.

- **Step 3: Alignment of Text.**
  - ➢ Choose the text that needs editing.

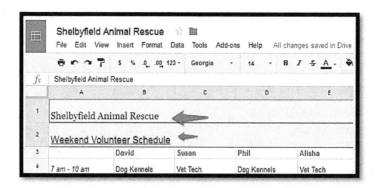

➢ Click on the horizontal alignment button that is in the Toolbar, you have to select your desired alignment from the drop-down menu.

You will notice that the text will realign as shown below

The Vertical Text Alignment Modification

After selecting the text you wish to change, click the Toolbar's "Vertically align" option. A drop-down choice will appear; select the alignment you want.

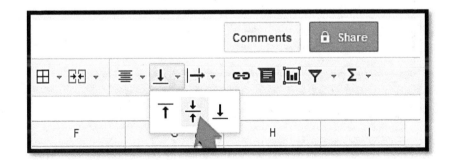

You will notice that the text will realign

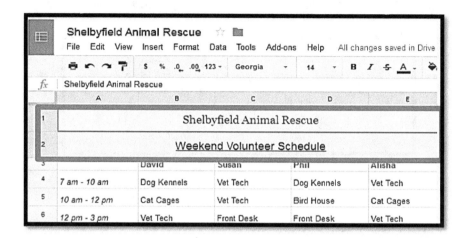

You can apply the horizontal and vertical alignment parameters to any type of cell when doing this.

Inputting background colors and cell border patterns

> ➢ Choose the type of cell or cells you wish to edit, then click Add Cell Boundaries.

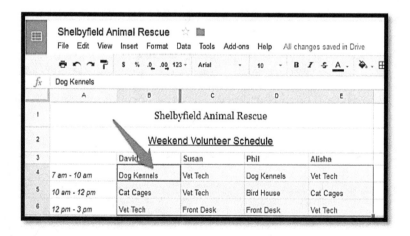

> ➢ Choose the borders button and then choose your desired border option from the dropdown menu.

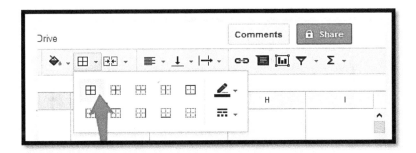

> The new cell will appear.

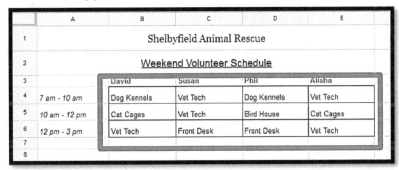

Editing The Color Of The Fill

You'll see that changing any cell's background color—also referred to as its fill color—is simple.

- Choose the cell or cells that you wish to edit.
- Find and click the fill color button located on the Toolbar.

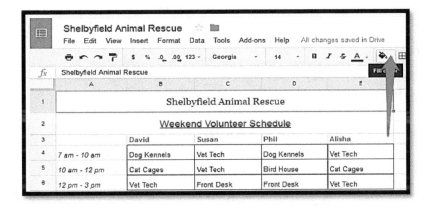

- Select a colour from the drop-down menu, here we chose blue as our colour.

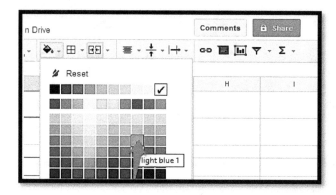

- When you finish choosing a colour, then the new fill colour will appear.

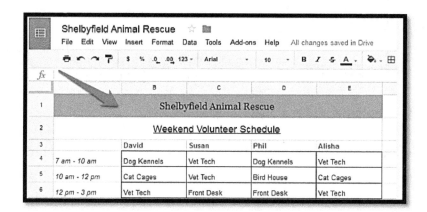

Applying formulas and carrying out calculations

Google Sheets can be used for a variety of calculations when working with numbers. You will learn how to write basic formulas in this section that you can use to multiply, divide, add, and subtract data. The fundamentals of using cell references in your calculations will be covered in this section.

The development of basic formulas

The fact that Google Sheets allows you to multiply, divide, add, and subtract other numerical data is one of its positive characteristics. The Google sheet may easily create and manage calculations by using mathematical expressions through formulas. We shall concentrate on formulas containing a mathematical operator in this portion of the book. Cell addresses will be mostly used in the calculation in this part. Cell referencing is the term we use for this. It has a benefit, which is that by employing cell referencing, the formula will immediately recalculate whenever a value is changed in the referencing cell. It will ensure that the values in your formulas are accurate when you employ cell references.

The operators in mathematics

The formulas on the Google sheet you are familiar with employ the standard operators. It employs an asterisk (*) for multiplication and a forward slash (/) for division in addition to the plus sign (+) and the minus sign (-) for subtraction. For exponents, a caret (^) is used.

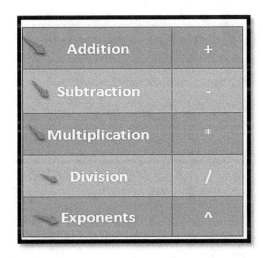

Every formula in a Google Sheet starts with the equal sign (=). This is due to the contents of the cells or what they equal when discussing the formula or the value that it computes.

Application of cell references

A formula is considered to be employing a cell reference if it contains a cell address. You should be aware of the benefits of developing a formula with cell references since it allows you to change all of the numerical values in the cells without needing to redo the formula.

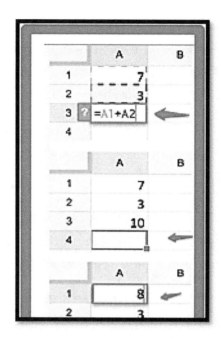

Each time you combine a mathematical operator with the cell references, then you can create a variety of simple formulas in Google sheet. You will notice that formulas are a combination of a cell reference and a number.

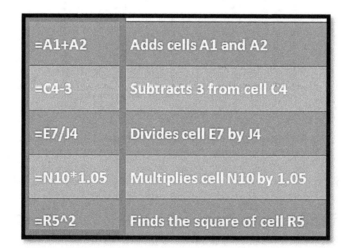

=A1+A2	Adds cells A1 and A2
=C4-3	Subtracts 3 from cell C4
=E7/J4	Divides cell E7 by J4
=N10*1.05	Multiplies cell N10 by 1.05
=R5^2	Finds the square of cell R5

Directions For Making Formulas

In the example below, we computed a budget using basic formulas and cell references.

Here's how to create the formula: choose the cell that will show your determined value, as indicated below.

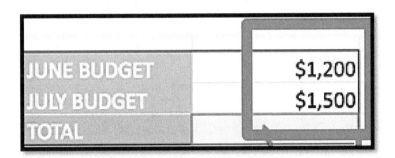

- You have to type the equal sign (=)
- You have to type the cell address that you want to reference in the formula. After you have done that, a dotted border will then appear around the cell that is being referenced.

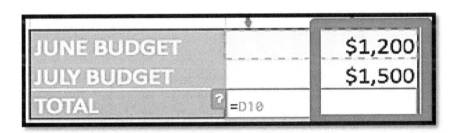

- Next, type in the operator you want to use. For example, you have to type the addition sign (+)
- The next thing to do is to type the cell address that you want to reference second in the formula.

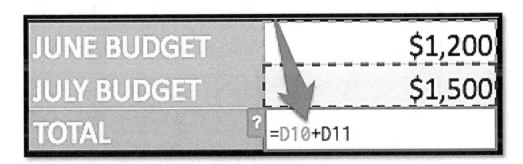

- You have to press the Enter key on your keyboard. The formula will be what will calculate while the Google sheet displays the result.

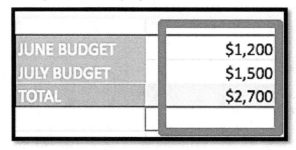

- If you want to see how the formula recalculates, you have to change the value in either of the cells. You will discover that the formula automatically will display the new value.

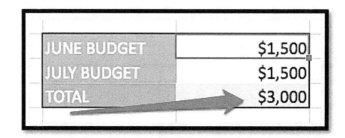

The Click And Point Method For Formula Creation

You can click and point at the cells you want your formula to include, saving you the trouble of entering in addresses.

- First, as indicated below, choose the cell that will show your estimated value.

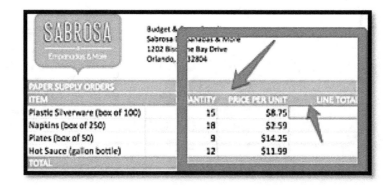

- Type the equal sign (=) When you have typed the equal sign, the next thing to do is to click on the cell that you want to reference first in your formula.

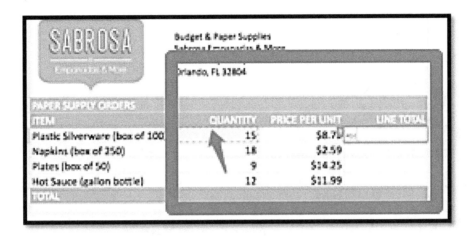

- When you have reached this stage, then you have to type the operator you will want to use in the formula. An example of this is when you type the multiplication sign (*)
- When this is done, then click on the cell you want to reference in your second formula. You will notice the cell will appear in the formula.

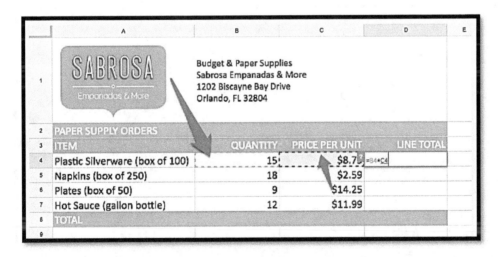

- Next, press the Enter key on your keyboard. You will notice that the formula will be calculated and the value will then appear in the cell.

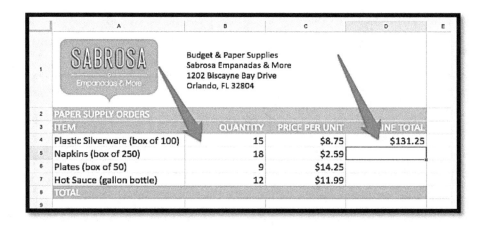

Modifying A Formula

One could state that, in terms of formula editing, there are situations where you would want to change an existing formula. This example has to be fixed because we choose to enter the wrong cell address.

- Double-clicking the cell containing the formula you wish to change is the first thing to do. The formula will be shown in the cell, as you will quickly observe.

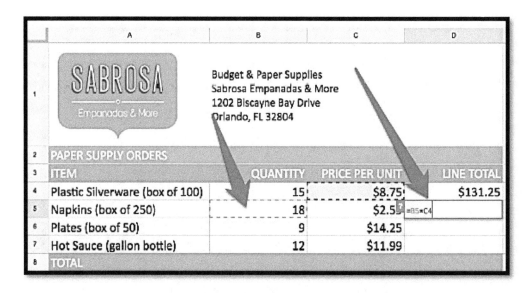

- Next, edit the formula. in the example below we replaced C4 with C5

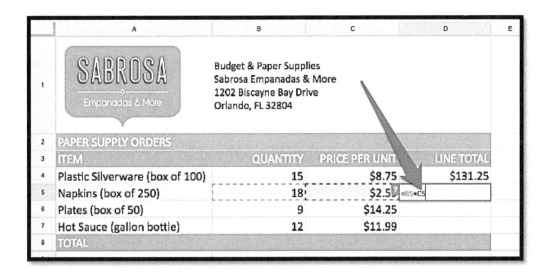

- Press the Enter key on your keyboard, you will find out that the formula recalculates and the new value will resurface in the cell

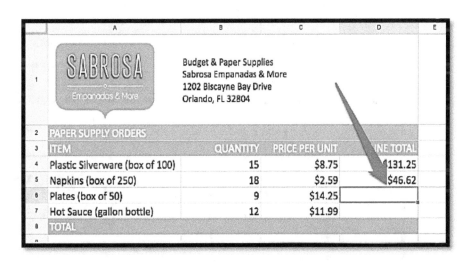

CHAPTER SIX

THE GOOGLE FORMS

These days, Google offers a lot of functionality. One interesting thing to note is that if you use Google Drive, you can build and email forms to friends and colleagues using Google Forms. One benefit of using Google forms is that you can compile all of your responses in one location. Additionally, you may include the form straight into your email.

Form-Making On Google

You have four options for creating a Google Form: the Forms website, your mobile device, Google Drive, or Google Sheets.

From The Webpage For The Google Form

- Visit forms.google.com and log in using your Google credentials.
- After completing that, select the Blank form with the + symbol.

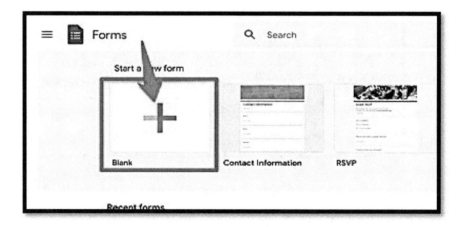

Using Google Drive

- Visit drive.google.com and log in with your credentials.
- Select Google Forms by clicking on New from the menu in the upper left corner.

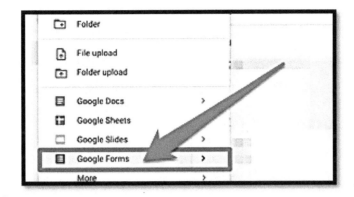

Based on the Google Sheets database:

Visit sheet.google.com, then create an account. Launch the spreadsheet of choice. After it is finished, select the form by clicking Insert.

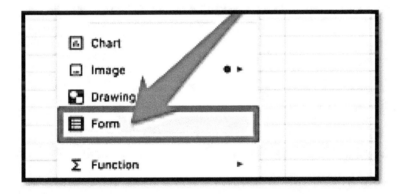

Using the mobile device

This will function. Whether it's an Android or iPhone doesn't matter. When you visit forms.google.com in an open web browser, such as Chrome or Safari, a new form will almost instantly appear.

How to Modify an Online Form

If you would want to obtain your paperwork, you have multiple choices. For instance, you can alter the questions, add pictures or videos, add sections or titles, and then modify the form's settings.

Including and modifying queries

- Once your form is open, select the editing option and make the necessary adjustments.
- You must utilize the Plus (+) symbol found in the form's menu on the right side in order to add a question. After that, decide what kind of question you want to add and start a new one.

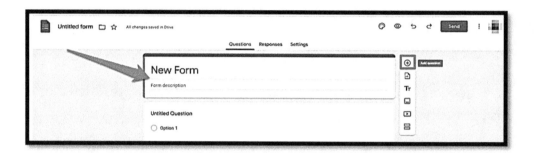

Including Pictures and Videos

- All you need to do is open the form, choose the portion or question you like to include in the media, and submit.
- To upload an image, click the image button located on the right side of the screen. From there, select the image by clicking on it.

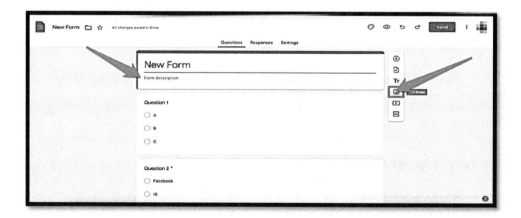

If you want to add a video, then click on the video icon in the menu which is on the right side of the screen. You have to choose your video and then you will hit the Select.

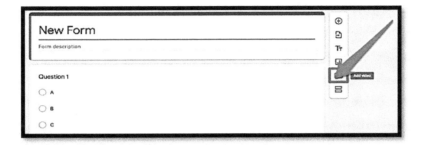

Including Section Headings

- Access your form now. Click the Title "Tt" option from the menu on the right side of the form if you would like to add a title.

- To add a section, you have to choose Add Section in the sidebar.

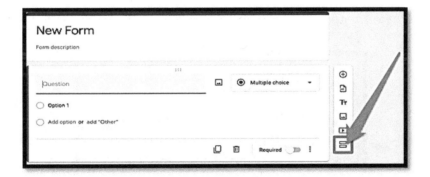

Personalized Google Form

Although Google Forms only allow for a limited amount of customisation, you should be interested in the fact that you can upload a header image and alter the theme, background, and font colors. You must use Formfacade and then add on for Google forms if you require further customisation.

127

Use The Theme Option To Customize Google Forms

- **Step one:** Click the adjust theme palette icon after opening your Google form.
- **Step two:** The theme option widget should now be visible to you. You should be aware that the default theme color is purple. You have the opportunity to create your own custom color or select another color from the list of alternatives. Everything is dependent on the theme color selected; four backdrop color possibilities will be displayed. You are free to select a color to use as the background of your page. Please take note that the form's color is fixed at white.

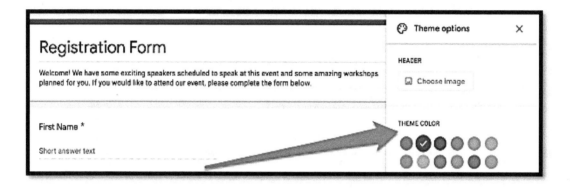

To add to this, you can upload a header image and then choose the font style. You must also note that there are only four fonts to choose from and they are as follows

- The basic
- The Decorative
- The forma
- The playful

If you require or need more customization options, then you use the Formfacade add-on for the Google Forms.

You have to be aware that Formfacade allows you to:

1. Put Google forms n your web page and you can make it look like your website theme.
2. Change your form layout -1 column, 2 columns, to fit the page
3. Customize the form background colours, font colours, and form elements.
4. Specify a font for a heading and then form elements.

Group Form Using Form Facade Add-On Customized

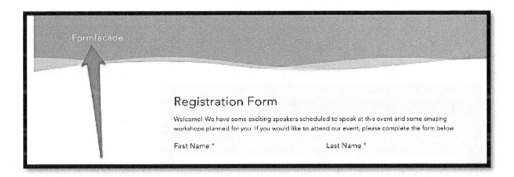

Displaying A Form

Once a form has been constructed and the appropriate options have been selected, sending it out is simple. Click the "Send" button to begin this process.

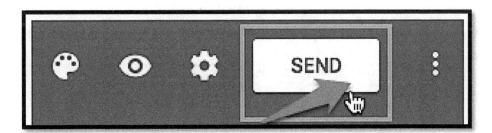

You will notice that this will bring out the send form menu. You must know that before sending your form, you have to decide on how you will send it out. You must also know that Google forms allow you to share the forms via email, the direct link, the embedding, and social media sites.

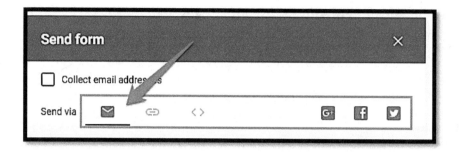

The one you select will rely on a number of things, such as your intended use of the form and the audience you are targeting. Let's examine the available choices and their potential applications. The ability to gather email addresses is what counts, not the specific approach you do. Your respondent will be asked for their email address when you turn it on; this will be useful if you want to get in touch with them quickly.

Transmitting Your Form By Email

Assuming you have the email addresses of everyone you wish to send the form to, this is probably the simplest way. To complete the form, simply provide all the necessary data and click the Send button.

Linking To Your Form And Sharing It

Email can be replaced with this. You can share the link to your form, created with Google Form, with anybody, anywhere. This is made so that when someone clicks on the link, your form will open immediately.

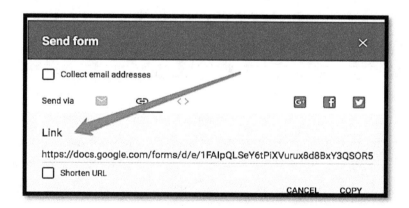

You can utilize this method, which you can transmit using text messages or any messaging app, if you have the email addresses of the individuals you want to send it to.

Embed - sharing your form

Using the embed option is better if you have a website where you would like to host the form. Usually, you will receive the HTML code from this, which you can copy and paste into a website editor such as WordPress.

Publishing Your Form On Social Media

As an additional option, you may share your form on social network. Social networking platforms like Facebook and Twitter allow you to share it. Click the button on the website you wish to utilize if you wish to share with a larger audience.

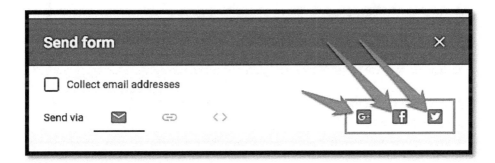

Looking at the Response

Once your form has been sent out and replies have been received, open your form and select the replies option to view these responses. The results of everyone who responded are there for you to see.

Putting your results in order with the Google Sheet

All of your answers are accessible within the form itself, although occasionally they may be challenging to go through and evaluate. The good news is that you can use Google Sheets to arrange your results into a spreadsheet by using Google Forms. You must click or press the spreadsheet icon in order to accomplish this.

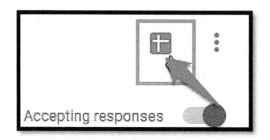

Once you do this, it will take you to where you can choose either to create a new spreadsheet or use the existing one.

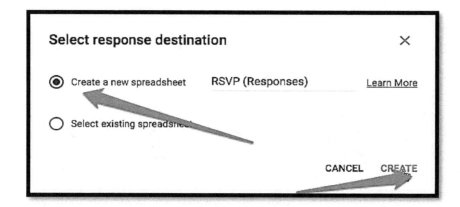

A spreadsheet will automatically be created and be opened in a new tab. Each of these rows will feature responses from each of the respondents while the column will feature a question from your form.

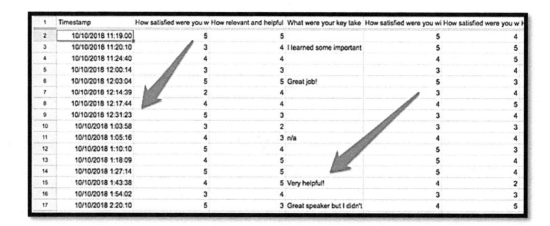

Google Sheets: How To Analyze Your Result

A spreadsheet could seem lovely at first, but Google Sheets tools will help organize things. One tool you can use to analyze your data is a formula. Simple calculations like addition and subtracting are carried out by formulas, but more complex calculations like averages and counts are carried out by functions. For example, you may wish to find out the average ratings that your employees hold for an even number. The ratings in a single column can be computed using the AVERAGE Function.

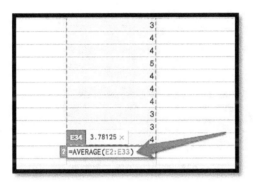

If you anticipate receiving more responses, it is preferable that you put your formula on a different sheet. You acknowledge that any additional responses will be appended to the end of the sheet you are now using. This complicates editing and formula discovery. When a lot of people respond to your form, the pivot table will assist you summarize the data. This will facilitate its manipulating ability. To build one, simply navigate to Data > Pivot table. The pivot table in the example below indicates the frequency with which each number appears to be selected for the query.

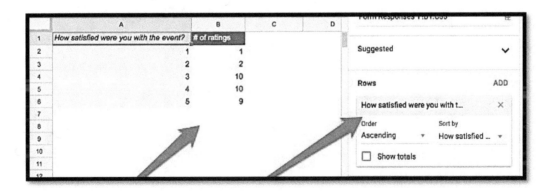

133

You may get a great summary of the responses you received with the help of the pivot charts and the histogram. Click Insert > Chart to start creating a chart. From the Chart Type drop-down list, choose the desired chart to use here. A pivot chart illustrating the distribution of attendees at your event is displayed in the example below.

CHAPTER SEVEN
ABOUT GOOGLE KEEP

Information may be easily organized with Google Keep. You may quickly scribble down ideas or share to-do lists with your colleagues in Google Keep. We'll be giving you advice on how to maintain your Google keeps in this part.

The first piece of advice is to "record your voice note" and store it on your iOS or Android device. You may do this by utilizing Google. Launch the Keep mobile app, tap the microphone symbol at the lower right corner of the screen, and record your message. Your recording will immediately stop when you complete speaking, and a new screen will appear with the text of your message and an audio file. After naming your note, click the audio file's title at the top. Your note and the web application automatically sync as a result. You can now access it on your desktop thanks to this.

You Can Transcribe Notes From Your photographs: It can transcribe text from photographs for you through the use of optical character recognition. We have a whiteboard session, so I don't have to bother about typing out my meeting notes. Simply snap a picture, choose "Grab Image Text," and you'll see that Keep is transcribing your message.

Drawing and Looking for Handwritten Notes: This allows you to scribble pictures in a notebook. You can view several settings by just selecting the symbol located at the bottom of your mobile device's screen. Play with hues, tints, and other elements. Once your drawing is complete, you can show it to your colleagues straight away. Alternatively, you can search for what you wrote and find your way back to the handwritten messages. When you look for words that contain images, you can find them. Imagine you take a picture of yourself at a whiteboard and discover that it has the phrase "Proposal" in it. All you need to do is look up "Proposal" on Keep; your photo should then show.

Notes From Keeps Are Dragged And Dropped Into Google Docs

The good news is that Google Docs has built-in support for keep. The notes you made in Keep can also be taken, dragged into client proposals, and used for other purposes. Recall that you should select "Keep Notepad" after selecting "Tools" from the menu bar if you are using Google Docs. All of your note selections will appear in a sidebar that appears. To find the exact note you need, use the search bar or scroll through the list. Once you've located it, drag it into your document and drop the message within. Recall that in order to send a note from the Keep app, you must first pick it, then select "Copy to Google Doc" from the three-dot menu. As an alternative, you can use Keep Notepad to take notes while you are viewing a document. The only benefit is that Keep generates a source backlink whenever you add a note in Docs. This implies that you can create the note in Keep and it will have a link to the original document that you produced it in.

Making Use of Chrome Extension

All it takes is downloading the Chrome Extension to start taking notes while you browse the internet. The best feature of this is that the URL of the website will be saved when you create a note using the extension. An added benefit is that the extension will display your note in context if you return to the same URL.

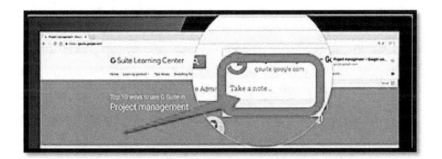

Transmitting Notes From Keeps To Other Apps You Use

You'll see that certain teams store stuff for future reference in keep from other chat or social networking apps. To share a note with another app, click the three dots in the lower right corner of the Keep app, choose "Send," and then choose whether to share it by email or another social network post.

Label or color-code your note to help you find it more easily

In order to color-code your notes in Keep, click the three dots menu at the bottom of the note and select a color from the available options. This will enable you to recognize a note quickly. If you would want to color code tasks or deadlines, you can use the Chrome Extension's Category Tab for Google Keep to assign category names according to color if you are working on a desktop. It will resemble the image below.

Organizing Reminders

To add reminders to a note, pick it and click the finger icon located in Keep's upper right corner of the screen. Recall that it contains a string. After doing that, a pop-up window with the ability to create reminders will appear. You will receive reminders in other Google products, such as the calendar, Chrome, and Android mobile device. In your Calendar app, under the "Don't see your Reminder" or "Switch between Task and Reminders" sections, you need confirm that the Reminders feature is turned on.

Taking notes

"What does Google retain?" It's essentially a free-form note-taking application. There were many debates and discussions over whether or not we needed another note-taking app when Keep was originally released and announced in 2013. People were contrasting the Keep with Evernote and other comparable products that same year. In the end, Keep has something all its own. Keep is a robust tool with a ton of functionality. Because Keep is so versatile, you can use it not just on the web but also on your PCs, Android apps, and iOS apps. It should be noted that since this is a Google product, it synchronizes with your

Google account. Furthermore, be aware that it is always current regardless of the device you are using. Additionally, it features a Chrome extension that makes adding and finding items simple.

Adding Color to Your Notes

Recall that Keep can get crowded with many types of notes when utilizing it. Once they are grouped, it can be difficult and uncomfortable to try to find what you're searching for if you leave it in the normal white color. You may start organizing things right away with the search function. Keep will help you stay organized because it lets you customize the color of your notes. Make all of your notes about work blue, all of your notes about eating green, and all of your notes about hobbies red, for instance. For example, you just scroll through and quickly look at the blue notes if you want to check on your work-related notes. To alter the note's color on the internet, simply click the palette button located at the bottom.

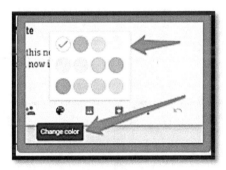

While on your mobile, tap on the three dots at the lower right corner and then select one of the colours at the bottom.

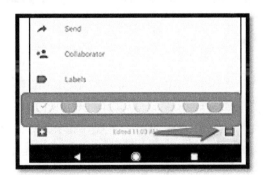

A Label For Your Note

To help you keep your notes better organized, you can add labels. Effective labeling can be a huge help when dealing with a lengthy and disorganized memo. Simply select Edit from your main menu, which is located next to the label choice. Here, you can change, add, or even remove labels.

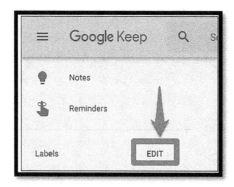

To add a label to your notes, you can tap on the menu button on the note and choose the "Add label " option. You can also type a hashtag directly in the note to open the label menu.

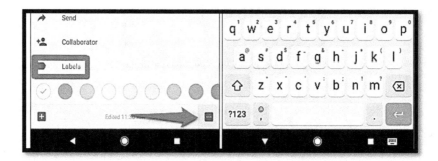

Organizing Reminders

Many people will always want to set location-based reminders for the tasks they want to do consistently and don't want to forget. One benefit of using reminders is that they help you stay focused on your future plans. It can literally save your life to receive a reminder notification. The most intriguing feature of those alert notification reminders is that location-based settings make them more effective. Location reminder will come in handy if you want to print your ticket at the library or question your boss about the increase in your pay when you get to the workplace. Receiving location-based reminders and notifications is a great feature, and you will learn how to set them up in this section.

The steps involved in creating location reminders in Google Keep for the web

The process of setting up location-based reminders for a new or existing note is much the same if you use Google Keep online. After selecting the note, click the Remind Me button in the left corner. When the reminder window is at its bottom, select Pick Place and type a location into the given box. Convenient suggestions will appear while you type. Simply select the appropriate location, then click Save. After viewing the location, you will choose the display that is contained in your note. Click the place, make your edits, and then click Save if you wish to make changes.

How to create location reminders in google keep on your mobile device

You should still make reminders on your Android or iOS device even though Google Keeps automatically syncs your notes and reminders. The reminders are sourced from the web and sent to your mobile device or wearables.

The actions to do that are listed below:

- You can either write a new note or choose an existing one and hit "Remind Me."
- If you're using Android, tap "Place," and if you're using iOS, tap "Pick Place."
- Type a URL, such as one you find on the internet, into the box. When you do this, some ideas will appear.
- After choosing the "right location," hit the "checkmark" button in the upper right corner.

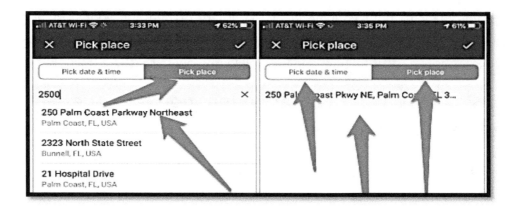

The precise spot you selected is now visible within your remark. All you have to do to make changes is to tap on the location, enter a new one, and then hit the checkmark to save it.

Notes for Sharing

You must consider working together with other employees or coworkers while sharing a note on Google Keep. A cloud-based note-taking program is called Google Keep. You can sync your notes across all of your devices with this software. Assuming you'll need to work together on a note, Google offers tools to make that possible. You will be able to share notes with other users or collaborators through this collaboration. You need to be aware that for collaboration to function, both of your collaborators' Google accounts must be active.

How To Use Google Keep To Share Your Note

Go to the note by opening Google Keep. You will see an icon at the bottom of the note. The Collaborator symbol, located second from the left, should be clicked. Enter the recipient's name or email address in the window that appears if you would like to work with them on the note. If you would like to work with more than one individual, you will need to write the email address or name first, followed by a comma, which will let you type an additional email address. Click Save once you have added every collaborator you wish to work with, and the note will be placed to their keep right away.

CHAPTER SEVEN
THE GOOGLE PHOTOS

The introduction of Google Photos took place in 2015. This software has the capacity to store screenshots, movies, and images. It functions similarly to a potent media backup that you can use. This is so that it can free up space on your phone, as it is a cloud-based tool. Some of the things you should be aware of about Google Photo's functionality are listed below.

The functioning mechanism of Google Photos

The benefit of Google Photos is that users may view, edit, save, and create new films, animations, collages, albums, and picture books in addition to uploading new images. You can choose for automatic backup and then sync your images and videos as soon as you take them if you don't own a Google device, such as a Pixel phone. If your phone is an Android, you have the option to restrict how much data you use for backups. This is done to ensure that when you are uploading files in the background, you never run out of data. Your images and movies can be preserved in a copy on Google Drive. You may accomplish this by selecting "Create a Google Photo Folder" from the Drive options, then clicking Save. Photos will be categorized as soon as they are added to your account. With this app's share feature, sharing pictures and albums is simple. If you have the "backup and sync" option fully enabled, this may occur. It's also noteworthy to note that, for a maximum of sixty days after deletion, you can still recover your data from the trash. Additionally, you can archive images to clear them out of the way while maintaining account searchability.

Free Unlimited Storage Asked Questions

The fact that Google Photos offers free, limitless storage is really intriguing. Whether you decide to save "highly quality images" instead of the original quality images will determine this. Naturally, you are aware that this may be a greater resolution. You should be aware that videos are compressed to 1080p and that the maximum picture resolution is 16MP. You can now approve auto-compression for uploads in the future. To accomplish this, navigate to settings and choose "high quality." You have the same option with your older pictures. All you need to do is select the "recover storage" option from the settings menu. You have up to 15GB of free space, which includes all of your drive's contents—photos, Gmail, and other files—if you'd like to stick with your original file sizes. If you would like, you can upgrade. The Google One subscription plan, which starts at $1.99 a month for 100GB, allows you to upgrade.

Among its features is an all-powerful assistant

Google Photos offers a plethora of automatically generated extras to its users. It can organize photos into groups and create a photo book collection, which is one of its intriguing features. This is determined by the date, the persons, and every location that was highlighted. Additionally, consumers have the opportunity to print their images and mail them. You need to be aware that the helper is capable of taking pictures that were shot quickly after another. They become GIFs as a result, and these GIFs are known as animation. Your pictures can be saved as motion pictures as well. This implies that they start and stop filming shortly before and after you take your shot. For iPhone users, it's known as live photographs.

its additional feature

Its extensive search feature is one of its platform's main draws. You can use it to look for general topics like "beach" or "dogs." This is merely a means of reducing your possibilities, which is beneficial, particularly if you have organized your photos into albums. You can choose how to identify various individuals in your images with this function. You accomplish this by giving each of their faces a name by hand. Once you've done that, the images of those people are automatically sorted, allowing you to later search for images of particular individuals. In a similar vein, you can make "live albums" that will automatically add pictures of your friends and family. You can scan and upload your physical photo prints if you want to back them up. They could use your phone or other devices to quickly snap a picture in order to accomplish this. You can highlight your favorite text in Google Photos if you have picture sheets. For added convenience, you can even crop off backgrounds when uploading and retrieving a receipt from a business trip. As you may have be aware, Google Photos is a strong and useful tool that may be used with some work. Without requiring you to remove your pictures or adjust the quality of your videos, it gives us limitless storage.

Image Interface

With the exception of the addition of its bottom bar in 2016, Google Photos' interface has not seen any significant changes since it was first released as a stand-alone application. On the other hand, the new account picker has just been introduced. This manifested as a revised user interface. This improves the bottom bar's intuitiveness and provides the eagerly anticipated functionality. The search bar at the top has been deleted and it has been redone in the new feature. This allowed for the removal of the hamburger menu and the creation of a much simpler Google Photos header. The familiar memories area, which displays your most recent photos further away, was placed after the top bar. The bottom bar has been rearranged, and the hamburger menu and search bar are no longer there. Photos, Search, For you, Sharing, and Library are the five items that have been added, up from the previous four. As a result, in order to search for photographs, we must navigate to a different tab. This highlights the near feature and is decidable.

One thing that stands out in this instance is that the keyboard doesn't open right away when you hit the search tab. You'll notice a few recommendations that are far more aesthetically beautiful than the ones we previously received with the previous UI. You'll see that the teasers for People and Pets include images. This is what set the new interface apart from the old one and made it much more beautiful. You will see particular search terms in the form of categories as you scroll down. These categories include "selfies," "screenshots," "videos," and many more. You may now quickly access the pictures you recently uploaded there thanks to this. You can even access the five-year-old photos you recently uploaded to your PC using it. In the past, in order to make them appear, you had to perform a URL hack on the Google Photos website. Remarkably, Google delivered on its promise when it included this app in its lineup of features.

As you can see, the album tab was eliminated in favor of the new library area, which still contains the same information. Along with collecting items from the old hamburger menu, this new library area also included garbage, device folders, archives, and other objects like utilities. As I mentioned before, the latter allowed you to use items like "Free up space" and "Manage your library," which were unavailable in the previous sidebar. There's a chance the picture book is there too.

It will become apparent to you that the interface may launch as a server-side upgrade. You are unable to immediately receive the new user interface. Because none of the Android Police have gotten it, it is a limited release.

Including images

Although Google has made significant progress in providing free photo storage, it recently stopped its photo-free storage program. You may still upload your pictures to the cloud because of the way it was designed. You will be able to submit your images by following these instructions. Google used to provide limitless free photo storage, but as of June 1, 2021, the maximum amount of free storage is now 15GB. All of the files on your Google Drive, Gmail, and Google Photos are included in this 15GB. You must choose Google One, a membership service, if you wish to upload files and pictures more than 15GB. There are four storage options available with Google One: 15GB of free storage A 100GB plan is equivalent to one pound fifty-nine pence per month, or fifteen pounds ninety-nine pence annually. A 200GB plan is equivalent to two pounds forty-nine pence per month, or twenty-four pounds ninety-nine pence annually. A 2 TB plan is equivalent to seven pounds ninety-nine monthly, or seventy-nine pounds ninety-nine annually. As of right present, there is no option for unlimited storage. If you require additional, you must consider other cloud storage choices. You are welcome to create more photo rooms if you so like. You can accomplish this by deleting big files from your Google Drive. You don't need to worry about the files that were already there as of June 1st since, if you don't pay, those images will have to stay on Google's servers and won't be removed or restricted.

Ways To Upload Google Photos Using Sync & Backup

To do this, download the Google Backup & Sync tool. After selecting a folder or folders to sync, you must wait for the images and any videos included within to be uploaded. You won't be able to choose the Backup & Sync or the root folder when you check and find that those directories are on Nas Drive. The basic remedy is to move all of your photo folders into a folder or folders that you create within that upload. The detailed instructions for installing Backup & Sync and uploading such photos to Google Photos are provided below. Please be aware that this only functions on Windows desktops. If you wish to upload photos from your phone, you will need to install the Google Photo app on your Android or iPhone. Click the download option after visiting your Google Photo page at https://photos.google.com/apps.

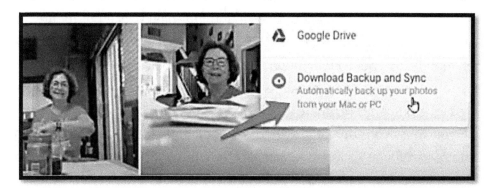

When you have downloaded it, click on your web browser or navigate to the folder where all the downloaded files were stored which is usually the downloads. Double-click on the file and get started.

You need to sign in to your Google account. I mean the one you are using for your Google photos

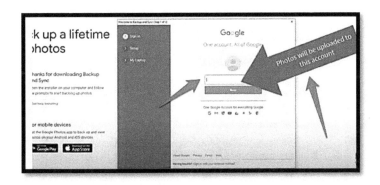

After viewing your designated screen, you will Make backups of your films and images. This is the point where you have to specify which folder your images are in Backup & Sync. To do this, click the box adjacent to the images. If your images are saved on an external disk, NAS drive, or another location, just click on CHOOSE FOLDER and go through the folders. Multiple folders can be synced, however you cannot select more than one folder at once. You must choose the desired quality from your stored photos and videos. As the file is compressed by your storage saver, you'll notice that it uses less space. The file cannot be compressed in the original quality, hence it will occupy extra space in your quota. After you click START, Backup & Sync will start uploading pictures and videos to the folders you've selected on Google Drive.

Sometimes, if you want to check on the progress, click on the symbol ^ which is on your Windows Taskbar, and click on the little white Cloud symbol. That's when you will see a scrolling list of files being as shown.

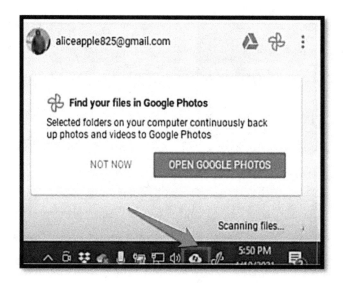

The overall quantity of data you are uploading as well as the upload speed of your internet connection—which is slower than the download speed—will determine how long it takes to upload all of your pictures and videos. While your laptop or computer is uploading the data, you should leave it alone. For instance, it took some users with a 16Mbps upload speed almost 24 hours to upload 30,000 images and movies from hundreds of folders on a network attached storage device. It is important to remember that the quantity of storage you have in your Google One account will determine how much you can upload.

Forming Album Section

The steps to build albums in Google Photos are as follows:

- Go to photos.google.com to access your Google account.
- When you get to the website, select "Albums" and then click the blue plus sign (+) that appears above "Create album."
- Choose an album name and click "add photos." You have two options: either drag and drop your image into the box or choose photos from your computer by

clicking "Select." Once you've chosen your pictures, click "Done" to share them with others.

Generating Albums In Mobile Google Photos

On your Android or iPhone smartphone, download the Google Photo app, sign in to your Google account, and then select "Albums" from the menu at the bottom of the screen. Next, you must hit the blue plus sign(+) that appears inside the "New album" box.

Enter the album name and then tap "Add photos" for you to select the images you want from your camera roll.

151

As soon as you're done uploading photos, you may choose to share your album or press the small back arrow located in the upper left corner of the screen. Where you made your album doesn't matter. The fact of the matter is that you can access your album from anywhere in the world, whether it is on a desktop, laptop, or mobile device.

The Publish Store

One of the greatest and most well-liked methods for storing digital photos is Google Photos. Their selection of print photos is growing. This includes placing an order for several hard copies of your most popular photos. Previously, for a monthly fee of just $7, Google Photos' delivery services would select the ten greatest images from your collection and deliver them to you. The distinction between then and today is that, although you could not select the kind of photos you would receive, you can now use an app to select which of your photos you would like to print, and you can purchase an infinite number of prints for just $0.18 each.

Prior to being able to order in sizes 4x6in, 5x7in, and 8x10in. If you were familiar with the Google Print Store previously, you will have noticed that four new print sizes—11x14, 12x18, 16x20, and 20x30—are now available. If you would like to provide snap-super in

152

an emergency, there is a chance for you. You can also place an order with your neighborhood store and have it delivered the same day. These retailers may include Walgreens, CVS, and Walmart.

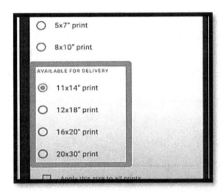

- **Google photo backup:** How you backup your snap with Google photo service.
- **Google photo vs Amazon photos:** Here you will know, which of these two Giants is the best?

How to get every photo from Google to your computer

Not only is the bigger print option a recent addition to Google in the US, but the company has also recently introduced a new canvas print option made with premium materials. As of the authoring of this book, Googe will be expanding its selection of canvas print sizes to include six more: 8x10, 16x16, 20x30, 24x36, 30 x40, and 36x36. The starting price for these sizes is $19.99.

The previous justification refers to the current Google Photo printing feature, which includes photo albums. These photo books are available in hard copy and soft copy, with prices starting at $9.99. This is also available as part of its current service, the premium printing series, and it costs $6.99 a month to have card stock images sent to your home. With its most recent product, Google suggests the greatest pictures of the month to you based on algorithms. It is currently only an option among the ever expanding print possibilities that the search giant itself offers. It's important for you to know that Google entered the photo printing market in 2018. 2018 saw the introduction of its first photo book service in the US. It began testing its AI-powered "Premium Print Service" prior to the pilot program's termination on June 30, 2020. The identical services recommenced in October 2020. Google has demonstrated that it will provide us with hard copies of the digital photos that it has saved on its cloud service.

Despite offering excellent services, Google is not the most affordable option for photo printing. While prints from Walmart and Snapfish cost less than ten cents each, Google's picture print store services offer a much more convenient option—printing straight from an app, which many users may also use to back up their phone images. Although Google Smart is not available anywhere, not even in more conventional photo print services, Google Premium Print Services offers Google smart features that have not yet been tested. Although Google can yet grow into other markets, such as metal and wood prints, their current market is undoubtedly an excellent place to start for the benefit of all users, especially business users. You need to be aware that whether it ends up in Google's cemetery of discontinued services depends on how brief their new print services turn out to be.

About Sharing

Google wants you to keep using their services because the more you use them, the more money the data firms can make off of you. Because I mentioned that Google wants you to keep using their apps, are you now discouraged? Because I mentioned that firms monetise your Google activities, do you feel like you are being used? Don't give up on yourself. Even though you can extract your emails, pictures, and other files from Googleverse, you will still gain more from it than from believing otherwise. I'll give you an example of what I'm attempting to explain as you try to figure out how these things work. Assuming you wish to share your family album—that is, the pictures of your family that you have saved in Google Photos—all you have to do is send them a simple link.

Directions For Viewing A Photo Album Online

To begin, select "Album" from the menu on the left. Then, move the cursor over the album you want to share and select the three dots. Following completion of that, select "Share album."

You can also accomplish this by clicking on the album in the upper left corner. To share an album, just select it and click "Share."

Sharing through the app for mobile photos

In the lower part of the screen, tap "Library". Next, choose "Share" after choosing the album you wish to share.

155

The Configurations

There are steps you must do to ensure your privacy settings are configured as you desire. To begin with, navigate to the album settings on your Google+ photo page. You can adjust your photo albums' privacy settings there. You can limit it to those who can view your pictures. Not everyone desires for everyone to see their personal or family photos. Certain individuals designate their photos for viewing by their family members, while others designate them for viewing by the families and close friends of those friends. Private settings are necessary since not everyone wants everyone to see their children's images. These options let you choose who may access your photos and how. The next steps are necessary for you to establish privacy settings on your albums. When you click Edit after selecting the album, a circle around your album with the words "Everyone or Limited" will appear. You can then type certain individuals and the circles that you want the album to be visible to when a pop-up box appears. Everything is up to you; if you want it seen by everyone, select "Public." You should be aware that you can select the circles you want to appear in the picture. You'll observe that the people you wish to see your album will be able to view it.

CHAPTER EIGHT
ABOUT GOOGLE KEEP

Information may be easily organized with Google Keep. You may quickly scribble down ideas or share to-do lists with your colleagues in Google Keep. We'll be giving you advice on how to maintain your Google keeps in this part.

The first piece of advice is to "record your voice note" and store it on your iOS or Android device. You may do this by utilizing Google. Launch the Keep mobile app, tap the microphone symbol at the lower right corner of the screen, and record your message. Your recording will immediately stop when you complete speaking, and a new screen will appear with the text of your message and an audio file. After naming your note, click the audio file's title at the top. Your note and the web application automatically sync as a result. You can now access it on your desktop thanks to this.

You Can Transcribe Notes From Your photographs: It can transcribe text from photographs for you through the use of optical character recognition. We have a whiteboard session, so I don't have to bother about typing out my meeting notes. Simply snap a picture, choose "Grab Image Text," and you'll see that Keep is transcribing your message.

Drawing and Looking for Handwritten Notes: This allows you to scribble pictures in a notebook. You can view several settings by just selecting the symbol located at the bottom of your mobile device's screen. Play with hues, tints, and other elements. Once your drawing is complete, you can show it to your colleagues straight away. Alternatively, you can search for what you wrote and find your way back to the handwritten messages. When you look for words that contain images, you can find them. Imagine you take a picture of yourself at a whiteboard and discover that it has the phrase "Proposal" in it. All you need to do is look up "Proposal" on Keep; your photo should then show.

Notes From Keeps Are Dragged And Dropped Into Google Docs

The good news is that Google Docs has built-in support for keep. The notes you made in Keep can also be taken, dragged into client proposals, and used for other purposes. Recall that you should select "Keep Notepad" after selecting "Tools" from the menu bar if you are using Google Docs. All of your note selections will appear in a sidebar that appears. To find the exact note you need, use the search bar or scroll through the list. Once you've located it, drag it into your document and drop the message within. Recall that in order to send a note from the Keep app, you must first pick it, then select "Copy to Google Doc" from the three-dot menu. As an alternative, you can use Keep Notepad to take notes while you are viewing a document. The only benefit is that Keep generates a source backlink whenever you add a note in Docs. This implies that you can create the note in Keep and it will have a link to the original document that you produced it in.

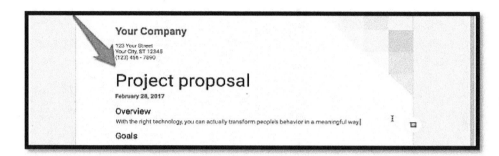

Making Use of Chrome Extension

All it takes is downloading the Chrome Extension to start taking notes while you browse the internet. The best feature of this is that the URL of the website will be saved when you create a note using the extension. An added benefit is that the extension will display your note in context if you return to the same URL.

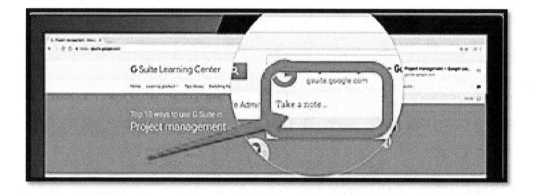

Transmitting Notes From Keeps To Other Apps You Use

You'll see that certain teams store stuff for future reference in keep from other chat or social networking apps. To share a note with another app, click the three dots in the lower right corner of the Keep app, choose "Send," and then choose whether to share it by email or another social network post.

Label or color-code your note to help you find it more easily

In order to color-code your notes in Keep, click the three dots menu at the bottom of the note and select a color from the available options. This will enable you to recognize a note quickly. If you would want to color code tasks or deadlines, you can use the Chrome Extension's Category Tab for Google Keep to assign category names according to color if you are working on a desktop. It will resemble the image below.

Organizing Reminders

To add reminders to a note, pick it and click the finger icon located in Keep's upper right corner of the screen. Recall that it contains a string. After doing that, a pop-up window with the ability to create reminders will appear. You will receive reminders in other Google products, such as the calendar, Chrome, and Android mobile device. In your Calendar app, under the "Don't see your Reminder" or "Switch between Task and Reminders" sections, you need confirm that the Reminders feature is turned on.

Taking notes

"What does Google retain?" It's essentially a free-form note-taking application. There were many debates and discussions over whether or not we needed another note-taking app when Keep was originally released and announced in 2013. People were contrasting the Keep with Evernote and other comparable products that same year. In the end, Keep has something all its own. Keep is a robust tool with a ton of functionality. Because Keep is so versatile, you can use it not just on the web but also on your PCs, Android apps, and iOS apps. It should be noted that since this is a Google product, it synchronizes with your

Google account. Furthermore, be aware that it is always current regardless of the device you are using. Additionally, it features a Chrome extension that makes adding and finding items simple.

Adding Color to Your Notes

Recall that Keep can get crowded with many types of notes when utilizing it. Once they are grouped, it can be difficult and uncomfortable to try to find what you're searching for if you leave it in the normal white color. You may start organizing things right away with the search function. Keep will help you stay organized because it lets you customize the color of your notes. Make all of your notes about work blue, all of your notes about eating green, and all of your notes about hobbies red, for instance. For example, you just scroll through and quickly look at the blue notes if you want to check on your work-related notes. To alter the note's color on the internet, simply click the palette button located at the bottom.

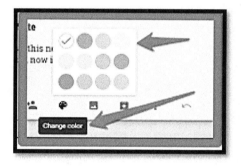

While on your mobile, tap on the three dots at the lower right corner and then select one of the colours at the bottom.

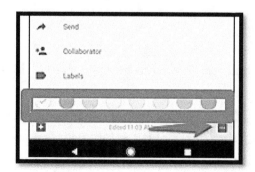

A Label For Your Note

To help you keep your notes better organized, you can add labels. Effective labeling can be a huge help when dealing with a lengthy and disorganized memo. Simply select Edit from your main menu, which is located next to the label choice. Here, you can change, add, or even remove labels.

To add a label to your notes, you can tap on the menu button on the note and choose the "Add label" option. You can also type a hashtag directly in the note to open the label menu.

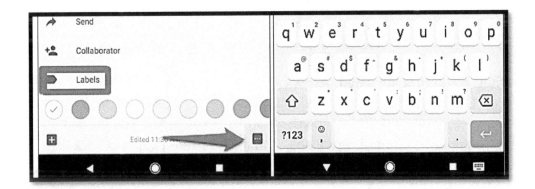

Organizing Reminders

Many people will always want to set location-based reminders for the tasks they want to do consistently and don't want to forget. One benefit of using reminders is that they help you stay focused on your future plans. It can literally save your life to receive a reminder notification. The most intriguing feature of those alert notification reminders is that location-based settings make them more effective. Location reminder will come in handy if you want to print your ticket at the library or question your boss about the increase in your pay when you get to the workplace. Receiving location-based reminders and notifications is a great feature, and you will learn how to set them up in this section.

The steps involved in creating location reminders in Google Keep for the web

The process of setting up location-based reminders for a new or existing note is much the same if you use Google Keep online. After selecting the note, click the Remind Me button in the left corner. When the reminder window is at its bottom, select Pick Place and type a location into the given box. Convenient suggestions will appear while you type. Simply select the appropriate location, then click Save. After viewing the location, you will choose the display that is contained in your note. Click the place, make your edits, and then click Save if you wish to make changes.

How to create location reminders in google keep on your mobile device

You should still make reminders on your Android or iOS device even though Google Keeps automatically syncs your notes and reminders. The reminders are sourced from the web and sent to your mobile device or wearables.

The actions to do that are listed below:

- You can either write a new note or choose an existing one and hit "Remind Me."
- If you're using Android, tap "Place," and if you're using iOS, tap "Pick Place."
- Type a URL, such as one you find on the internet, into the box. When you do this, some ideas will appear.
- After choosing the "right location," hit the "checkmark" button in the upper right corner.

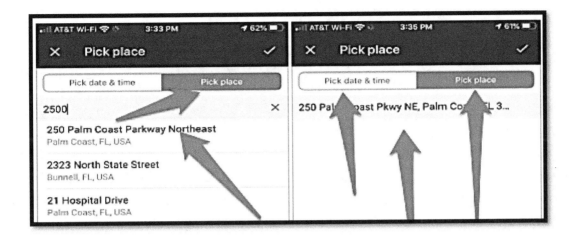

The precise spot you selected is now visible within your remark. All you have to do to make changes is to tap on the location, enter a new one, and then hit the checkmark to save it.

Notes for Sharing

You must consider working together with other employees or coworkers while sharing a note on Google Keep. A cloud-based note-taking program is called Google Keep. You can sync your notes across all of your devices with this software. Assuming you'll need to work together on a note, Google offers tools to make that possible. You will be able to share notes with other users or collaborators through this collaboration. You need to be aware that for collaboration to function, both of your collaborators' Google accounts must be active.

How To Use Google Keep To Share Your Note

Go to the note by opening Google Keep. You will see an icon at the bottom of the note. The Collaborator symbol, located second from the left, should be clicked. Enter the recipient's name or email address in the window that appears if you would like to work with them on the note. If you would like to work with more than one individual, you will need to write the email address or name first, followed by a comma, which will let you type an additional email address. Click Save once you have added every collaborator you wish to work with, and the note will be placed to their keep right away.

CHAPTER TEN
THE GMAIL

Google launched Gmail on Thursday, April 1st, 2004, ushering in the contemporary era of the web. The development and popularity of Google Mail has greatly contributed to the modernization of the online, making this the modern era of the internet. People were so accustomed to Microsoft Hot Mail before the introduction of Gmail. When Google arrived in 2004, webmail was completely eclipsed. Gmail has gained so much traction that almost nobody in the world is unaware of its existence. With Gmail, you can send and receive emails, store files, send pictures, and much more. Seldom does someone who utilizes the internet not have a Gmail email account. While sent mail from other webmail providers typically takes longer to arrive. The majority of individuals in African nations only know Gmail as their email address. Google has quickly completed the line after picking up the mantle from other webmail services provided by other corporations.

A day before its official launch, rumors circulated that Google was going to start providing free email services. This information was welcomed by a large number of individuals. At the time, the story was originally reported by Markoff Joh of the New York Times. This was really amazing because it was shocking to think that the search engine KingPin was launching email services, and everyone was waiting to learn about the 500 times larger storage capacity than Microsoft Hotmail. Many who were supporters of Google services welcomed the news when it was announced by Google on April 1, 2004. Those who had doubts about their claim that Google was offering a free gigabyte subsequently discovered that it was a revolutionary and true claim. Google's historic 1998 launch has caused a stir around the globe. I can assure you that Google not only outperformed Yahoo and Hotmail in webmail, but it also took the lead in the industry. Prior to its launch, the only email services that were widely used were Yahoo Mail and Hotmail. However, I can assure you that its superior capabilities, including immediate search, fast interface, and ample storage, are unmatched. Google is the main cloud-based application that has the ability to replace traditional PC software; this is not a complementing relationship; rather, it is a takeover that is anticipated to occur in the near future.

Talking about Google is synonymous with talking about Gmail. Gmail was thought to be a very unlikely thing. Three years passed before the product was able to be purchased by customers. It needs to realize that nothing new is simple, as cynical Google employees exposed the idea of several levels of explanation—from technical to philosophical. Have you ever imagined a different reality in which everything failed miserably or turned out to be far less fascinating, and then introduced Google? It will get more engaging, in my opinion. When Google was launched, George Harik, who was in charge of the most of the company's new products, remarked, "It was a pretty big moment for the internet."

Google Originated As A Search

The result of Google's 20% effort is Gmail. Their engineers can allocate a portion of their work hours to their projects thanks to a fabled policy. I can confirm that this idea was published by Mr. Paul Buchheit. He said, "It was an official charge, I was supposed to build an email thing" . He began working for Google in August 2001, having previously had a bad job before joining the company in 1999 as its twenty-third employee. "I had started to make an email program before in, probably 1996," he suggested. He continued to elaborate, saying, to quote, "I worked on this idea for a few of weeks until I grew bored. I wanted to construct web-based email. One thing I took away from it was the psychological necessity of constantly having a usable product. Building something helpful and then continuously enhancing it is my first action on a first-day basis. You should be aware that the initial code name of Gmail was caribou. It was an adopted moniker. From his email, Buchheit constructed its helpful search engine. It took him a full day to finish. He completed another project or piece of work on Google Groups. The illustrious Usenet discussion groups were indexed by Google Groups. All he needs to do is leverage the Group's blazingly quick search function and direct it to his email rather than Usenet.

First, there was a server on Buchheit's desk that housed the email search engine. He took special care to get input from engineers, and to his astonishment, they suggested that it search their messages, which is exactly what happened in the end. The primary function that Google introduced with its search engine was considerably superior to anything provided by the big email services, and thus ensured that their reputation was formed. They reasoned that an industrial-strength search would be necessary if they had to match Hotmail's capability.

Their thorough investigation needed to ask for thorough storage. This gave you the option to save all of your emails indefinitely as opposed to deleting them in order to stay under the quota. They decided to give each user 1GB of space as a result of this. After considering capacities that were generous rather than absurd—imagine something as small as 100MB—Google needs to sort this out. Many said that it was a poor decision and a lousy strategy from a strategic and product standpoint. Prior to deciding to offer its consumers a free 1 GB of space, Google made the decision that the product will be available for purchase. It appears to have been a poor brain work despite its insane email-centric culture. When Google first started out, its obsession with and focus on its search engine was what made it stand out from companies like Yahoo, Excite, Lycos, and other pioneering search competitors who rebranded themselves as "portals" and expanded their ambition to include everything from email to sports, games, and weather. It's commonly known that the gateways work together to accomplish a lot of things, although not always successfully. What actually happened was that many people believed it to be a poor product and strategic plan. They were worried that it had nothing to do with searching the internet. Some expressed fear that other businesses might take advantage of this and lie to Microsoft in order to destroy them. The fact that the founders were not among the skeptics is a good development. Before other engineers joined him on this project, Bucheit had been working on it for two months. The Gmail team or staff has expanded over time from its 2004 size.

From his first day at Google in 2002, Brian Rakowski—the original product manager of Gmail—learned a lot about customer service from his manager, Marrisa Mayerright. Fresh out of college, he was impressed and became excited by what he witnessed. He continues to work on Android for Google today.

How Gmail Appears

Unlike Hotmail and Yahoo Mail, which were launched in the middle of the 1990s, Gmail is more of an app than a website. My experience with Yahoo and Hotmail was that they required a complete page reload each time you tried to access them, and they were slow to load. Mr. Buchheit used highly interactive JavaScript programming to work around HTML constraints. Because of this, it felt less like a collection of web pages and more like software. The web browser wasn't so great back then, thus many individuals opposed their aspirations regarding Java Script. They were worried that users wouldn't want to continue using it if browsers crashed.

Over time, he observed that Gmail's capabilities increased with the amount of JavaScript it used. One of the things you'll notice about its flagship is that messages didn't always appear in your inbox in a perfectly consecutive order. You'll see that all of the messages were relatively difficult to understand and were moving back and forth, rather than the intended easier-to-follow discussion threads. Overtaking Yahoo, Hotmail, and other former online tech behemoths, Gmail has emerged as the dominant global webmail service. For the most part, it has connected people from all over the world financially. The majority of their product offerings generate enormous profits, and if Google keeps heading in the same direction—businesses are starting to favor Google Docs over Microsoft Word, and Google Docs offers services that are exclusive to Google—it will eventually surpass Microsoft.

The Gmail Interface

To improve the comfort and usability of the Gmail console, Google unveiled a new Gmail user interface. We'll talk about this new interface in this section, and they are:

- Organizing email from your inbox
- Snoozing your emails
- Nudging options
- Viewing Calendar, Task, keep add-ons from Gmail. Organizing emails from your inbox

Sorting through your mailbox of emails

The new functionality lets you organize emails directly from your inbox. Whether you wish to read, snooze, delete, or archive is irrelevant. To complete the task, simply drag the mouse pointer to the right side of the email and click where necessary.

169

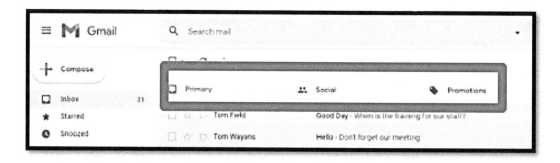

Snooping through your mails

You may choose to snooze your emails at the time of your choosing by using this feature. In other words, it takes time to work. When you choose this option, which is located at the upper right corner of the screen, you can adjust the timing.

Option for nudging

There is a feature in the Gmail interface that allows you to choose not to respond to any emails. By bringing them back to the front of your inbox, the Nudging option recognizes this type of communication. Using the same Gmail window to view the calendar, tasks, and add-ons. The Calendar, Task, Keep, and Add-ons are all in the same window, so you don't need to click on any more windows. You must locate it on the right sidebar and click on it once in order to access it. If you would want to use them, you can choose to add certain add-ons; they are located on the right side of the bar.

Browse Categories

Google has made significant improvements to its email layout and categories. Gmail allows you to organize your inboxes into tab-based categories. Primary, Social, Updates, Forums, and Promotions are the categories. Gmail may sort emails into tabs based on the following categories, allowing you to focus on the ones you want to read. Your emails are automatically categorized by Gmail, regardless of whether you use the tabbed view or not.

Ways To Activate The Categories Inbox Tab

After selecting all of the settings by clicking on the settings menu, you must select the inbox tab and confirm that it is set to Default. Once that's done, click the save changes button at the bottom of the page and check the box next to the categories you want to see in your inbox tab.

The Various Categories Available

- **Primary:** This is a conversation between two people. Messages that are not visible in other tabs are shown here.
- **Social:** These are communications from social media websites, online dating services, media sharing websites, and other social networks.
- **Promotions:** These include political and social media pages, marketing emails, and other promotional materials.
- **Updates:** These are self-generated, personal updates. These consist of invoices, confirmation, bills, and further statements.
- **Discussion boards,** mailing lists, and other online groups' posts can be found in forums.

Training Gmails To Transfer Emails To Another Tab

To relocate the messages, right-click on them, select the relocate to tab, and then select the desired tab. There will be a notification that shows up in your window's lower left corner. It will inquire as to whether you want to process all emails sent from that address. If that's what you want, click Yes.

Working On A Filter To Transfer Emails To Another Tab

You can choose to Filter messages similar to these by clicking the three vertical dots icon directly within your email. Before clicking "Create filter," verify sure the address in the form box is correct. Select the category to which you wish to move it after checking the Categorize as a box. To have your current message recategorized, tick the Apply filter to [#] matching discussions box below. After completing it, select "Create filter."

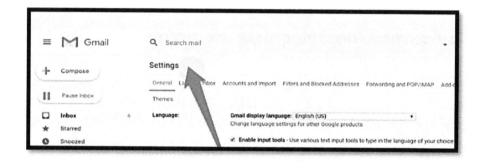

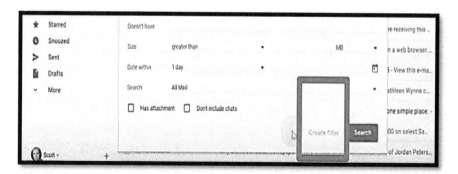

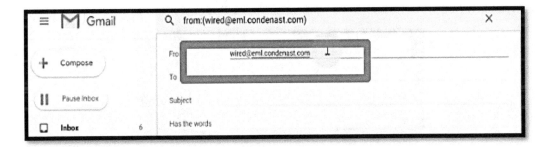

Ways To Offset Unwanted Tab

- Click on settings.
- Click on the inbox tab.
- Uncheck the category or the categories you will like to disable.
- Click on the Save Changes at the bottom of the page.

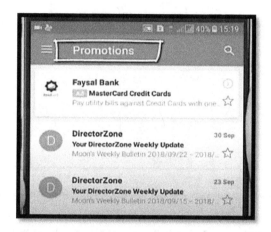

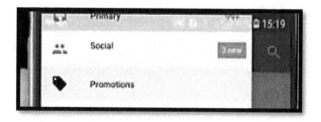

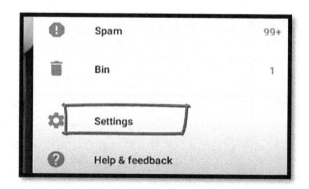

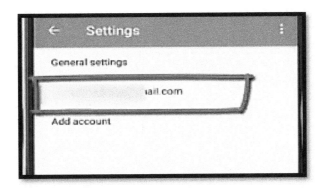

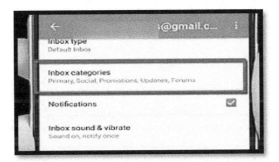

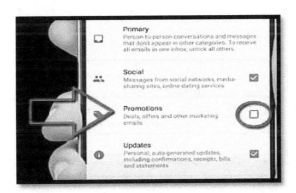

Email Sent And Received

- Open up your computer and then select a browser.
- Log in to your Gmail account.

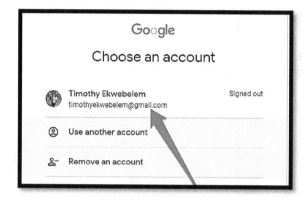

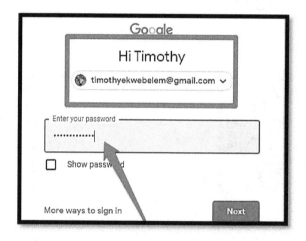

- Simply click the compose button in the upper left corner of the new page.

- You will notice the appearance of a box on the screen an empty field, here add the recipient address (You can add other recipients in the Cc and Bcc field).

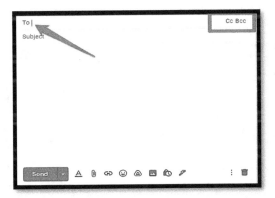

- Write the subject after typing the email address.

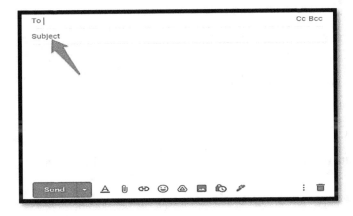

- You will see an empty page for the body, write your message.

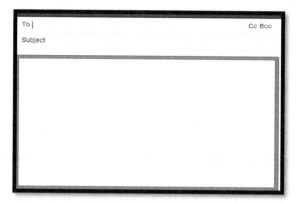

- The send option is at the bottom of the page, just click Send when you're done writing your email.

Oversighting Spam

Although Gmail has an excellent system in place to manage your junk mail, occasionally you will still receive these unsolicited emails. You will discover how to prevent them from reaching your mail inbox in this section.

Why are unwanted message accessible in your inbox?

Unwanted communications come from two sources, which are:

The people you know and the people you don't know: You do receive unsolicited communications from individuals you know when you quit a project or a job. They are still sending you emails, most likely because they have your email address on file and it is connected to your previous employment.

Emails from strangers can occasionally arrive in your inbox. These correspondences are undesirable as you don't know the sender and have no business dealing with them.

Spammers are those who obtain email addresses through the methods outlined below.

- **Speculation:** Occasionally, they employ algorithms to produce different versions of your emails. They send spam messages to everyone whose email address they obtain, or to any email they create.
- **Hacking:** Occasionally, even secured lists are breached, exposing your personal information, including email addresses.
- **Purchase:** It should come as no surprise that some businesses provide email address lists for sale. When you reply to their free offer, they can obtain your email   address.

  Scraping: Spammers can utilize technologies to look up every email address that has been publicly disclosed online. They use publicly posted web emails to deliver spam messages to the email addresses they own.

Methods For Filtering Messages From Particular Senders

First Method: The message you wish to block must first be open from the sender. In the upper right corner of your screen, click the downward arrow. Choose the "Sender Name" block option. A confirmation notice stating that mails from that specific sender will now be seen as spam will be sent to you. The following time, his or her mails will end up in the Spam folder. To validate the message, click the Block button after that.

Setting An Account

It's really simple to set up Gmail. To begin, create a Google account. During the rapid account setup, select an account name. You will find instructions for creating a Gmail account in this section. To register, visit www.gmail.com.Next, open the account. You will see the sign-up form; fill it out according to the instructions.

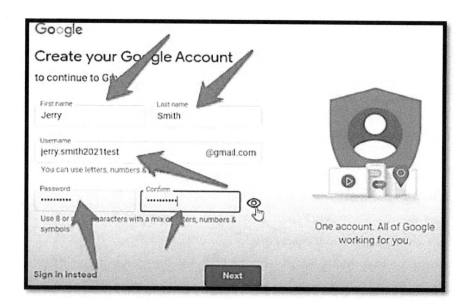

The next step is to enter your phone number to verify your account. Google uses a two-step verification process for its security.

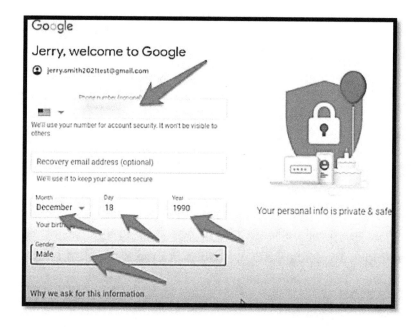

You will receive a text message from Google with a verification code. You have to enter the code to complete the account verification.

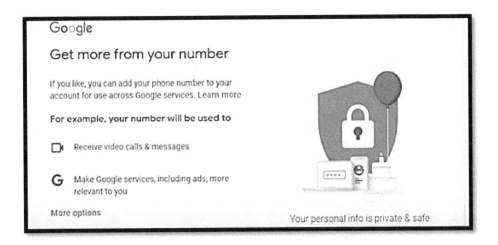

You will have to review Google's terms of service and privacy policy and click I agree.

At this moment your account has been created and you are right in the Gmail interface inbox.

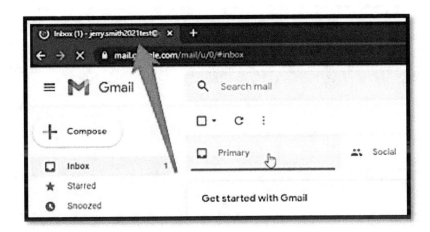

Including An Event

Open the message in Gmail and select the three-dot icon to add an event. If your computer has a keyboard shortcut for Gmail configured, you can also press the period key.

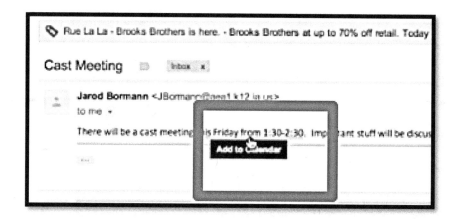

Select the create event to open the Google calendar. You must know that the Google calendar populates the event name with the subject line of the email. You have to select a date, start time, and the end of time. This you will get from the drop-down menus which are under the name of the event which is at the top of the screen that is if they do not transfer from the email. Repeat at regular intervals if it is an all-day event and then make your required choices.

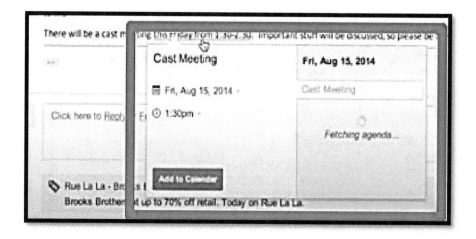

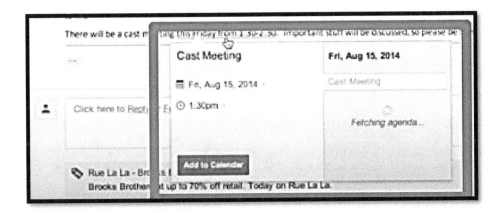

You need to add a location for the event.

Set a notification that will remind you about the event at a particular time.

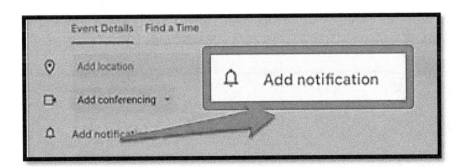

- At this stage, assign a colour to indicate if you will be busy or free during the event.
- Click on save to the event on your calendar. However, if you want to adjust the changes on your event in the calendar you will need to click on the pencil icon on the screen.

183

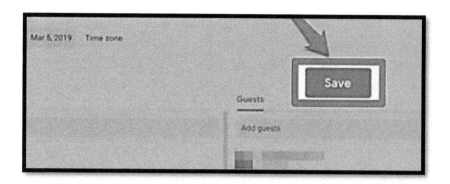

About reminder

After opening the email, select Settings. Navigate to the "Nudges" section by scrolling down while in the General app. Next, select "Suggest emails to reply" and "Suggest emails to follow up" once again.

About Task

You may create a task in Gmail by navigating to the Task, Calendar, and other Google app icons on the right side of the screen. If it's not visible, look for a tiny arrow in the lower right corner of your screen. This arrow will allow you to reveal or conceal the side panel. You need search for the Task's icon inside the panel if you wish to open it. A blue button with a white line and a yellow dot will be visible. Click it to access Task from the right-hand sidebar. Next, select "Add a task" to start the task creation process.

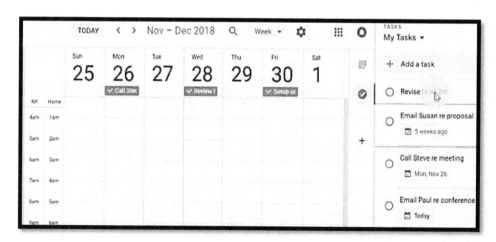

You will have to enter the task at the place it says "Title". You can as well enter the details of the task and then set a date and time.

Click the task name, details, and date to edit or add more to it. You can also click the three dots to the right of "Add a task" to change the sort order or delete a task. To add a subtask or make general changes to your task list, click the three dots to the right of "Groups" and tasks.

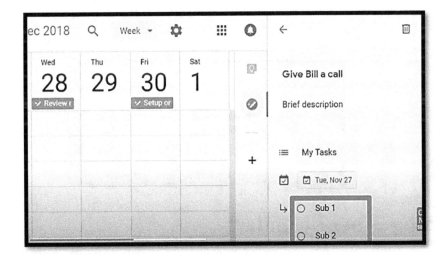

To change the order, all you have to do is to drag and drop the task if you want to save an email a task, drag the email into the Task sidebar.

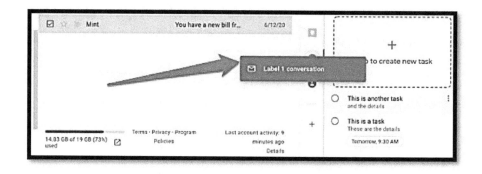

If you want to mark a task complete, click on the circle on the left of the task.

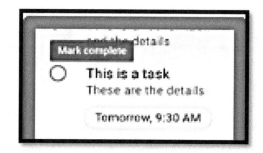

If you want to view your completed task, click on "Completed" which is at the bottom of the sidebar.

Including Other Calendars

You can use the instructions below to add more calendars to your Gmail account. Click the setting icon when you have opened your Google Calendar account, and then select "Settings." Navigate to alternative calendars, then scroll down to locate the public address in iCal format. Once you find it, copy the URL.

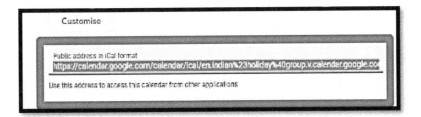

The next thing is to go to your browser, then paste the link in the search bar and download an "ics" format file. You have to go back to the Google Calendar and open the settings again and then go to "Add Calendar" below general.

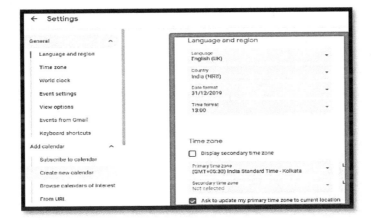

You then have to create the new Calendar and fill in the name and the description of the calendar.

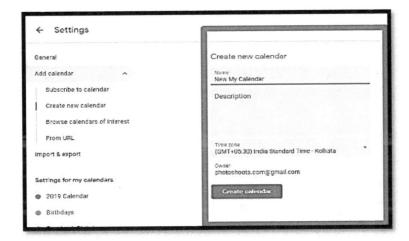

Look for the "Import & Export" section and then import the downloaded .ics (iCal) format from your computer. After doing that choose the new Calendar you want the file to be imported to.

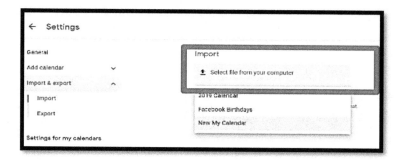

Configurations

Regarding webmail, Google has accomplished a great deal. One of the most effective email programs out there is Gmail. One problem about Gmail is that its configuration pages are thick with applications, hiding many of its features.

You must modify the undo send limit

Gmail gives you five seconds by default, during which you can send an email. As you are aware, this usually provides you enough time to realize if you neglected to attach anything, allowing you to retrieve the email. To extend the duration of this window, navigate to Settings > See all Settings > undo send. From there, you may increase the duration to 30 seconds. You can stretch it to a point where you have just enough time to fix your errors.

Verifying actions on a mobile device

It is quite simple to tap in the incorrect areas, delete the wrong email, or even reply before you're ready when using a mobile device to check or reply to emails. The Gmail app has the advantage of requesting confirmation before taking certain activities. To verify before deleting, archiving, or sending emails, navigate to Settings > General Settings > Action Confirmations in your mobile Gmail app. Before sending the email, Gmail will ask you to confirm that you are confident about the option you have selected.

The symbol for unopened messages

Enable the "Unread message icon" by going to options > See all options > Advanced. This will cause your Gmail tab's icon, which displays your number and the number of unread emails you have, to be updated. It will refresh when a new email arrives. This is especially helpful if you want to keep track of every email you get without having to open Gmail to check your inbox size.

Enabling more than one star

Do you know that Gmail includes a rating system? Go to Settings > See all Settings > Stars to enable them. You can find a variety of stars and icons here that you will want to include in your rotation. Select one by dragging it from "Not in use" to "In use." You must now apply for the normal star whenever you click on the star icon in Gmail.

Archiving and sending with just one click

Go to Settings > See all settings>General, then enable "Send and Archive" if you want to send emails without having to click on them every time. This means that when you use your default send button, it will send both emails and simultaneously archive your chat.

Personalized Keyboard Shortcut

You'll discover that one of the greatest time-saving tools is the Gmail shortcut. You have to be aware that they are not limited to default settings. To modify your shortcut for greater workflow convenience, navigate to Settings > See all settings > Advanced, then select "Custom keyboard shortcuts." To have the modification take effect, you need to click "Save changes" and then reload Gmail. As soon as you return to the Settings page, a new tab labeled "Keyboard shortcuts" will appear. The current shortcuts from your extensive lists of possible Gmail operations are located here. It's likely that the most of them already have a keyboard shortcut assigned to them. You have the option to add another custom shortcut or to go with the default. Before you ever use any new shortcuts, you have to be sure they won't interfere with the ones that already exist.

CHAPTER ELEVEN
ABOUT CONTACTS

One of the most potent contact management tools available is Google Contacts, one of the many amazing things Google has accomplished with its app development. One of the key components of the Google suite of online applications is Google Contacts. How does it function? It keeps track of and arranges your contact details for both business and private use. This is important information for you to know, particularly if your company uses Gsuite, which comes with a Gmail server. In that case, you can use Google Contacts as a repository. This software is compatible with other Google apps and is available for free. It is well-liked and a good option for other small enterprises in need of a straightforward, reasonably priced application for managing their personal and commercial contacts.

How To Use Google Contacts

You may be surprised to learn that Google contacts maintains your Gmail account up to date and organized in the background. Your network consists of more than just your address book. In order to help you manage and arrange your contact information, Google Contacts has developed to include a multitude of information fields and segmentation possibilities. Both your phones and email inbox are included in this. You should be aware that contacts from your Gmail account are immediately added to your Google contacts. Despite being linked via Gmail, you have the ability to manually edit, enhance, and add new contacts. Additionally, you should be aware that your basic information is included in each of your contact records. Name, last name, phone number, and company are some of your essential details. You can use this to add notes to any of your contacts and to categorize or distinguish your contacts into groups. It is also important for you to understand that labels, which group contacts into categories like "New lead," "Prospects," and "Customer," are very helpful for your business. Finally, you should be aware that labeling contacts in Google Contacts that you have both personal and professional relationships with will help you avoid confusing them.

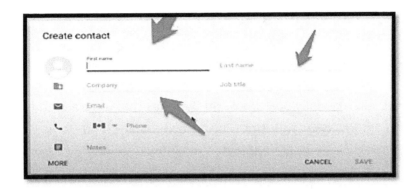

You can add a variety of information, such as a prefix, suffix, nickname, birthdate, and more, to your contact records by clicking the "show more" button in the bottom left corner. If you would like, you have the option to create a custom field for your contacts.

Management Tips For Your Contacts

Labels were mentioned in this part, and I also hinted at the process of adding a contact to your Google contacts. On the left side of the pane or sidebar on your Google Contacts homepage, the label will show up. You want to know how many contacts are in each group so that you can quickly see which contacts belong in which group.

You will also be able to see an overview of all the contacts that you have contacted frequently, other contacts, and contacts that you have merged or fixed the least, to supplement the visualizing labels.

Other Contacts As Well As Yours

You can see that there is a "See contacts" option on the left side of the bar in the screenshot, and there is also an additional "Other contacts" option at the bottom. The contacts that you manually uploaded and the ones that were added to Google via an integration or contact sync will both be shown when you look at the Contact. Google automatically saves email addresses in other Contacts groups when you send someone an email but haven't added them as a contact yet. The next time you wish to email them, you'll see that their email addresses will just appear on your Gmail account automatically. Their "autocomplete" feature is what causes that to happen. To transfer connections from Other contacts to contacts, just pick the contacts you wish to move, then click the Add contacts button located above the list.

You can turn off this function if you don't want every contact in the email saved to Other contacts. Navigate to your Gmail account and select Settings from the menu in the upper right corner. All you need to do is choose I'll add contacts myself when in the Create Contact for Auto-Complete area, and then click Save Changes at the bottom.

Integration Of Contacts

Duplicate contacts cannot be located in Gmail or Google Contacts. This implies that a single person may be listed in multiple contact records that you have. Because every one of their records is kept independently in informational fragments, you are unable to duplicate them. Gmail's most intriguing feature is its ability to integrate or repair contacts with Google. When Gmail finds contacts that might be duplicates, it automatically flags them and displays them under the Merge and Fix option on the left-hand menu. These contact records are available for your assessment, and if you'd like, you can even merge or amend them. As an illustration, consider the possibility that you added the same contact to Google Contacts more than once. In some cases, you may have added the contact with their phone number but not their email address, or vice versa. If you select the Merge and Fix option, you will see the entries for both contacts. As such, it gives you the option to choose whether to combine the two inputs into one. All you have to do is click Merge, and your duplicates will be removed. If you need to make any changes to your contacts, this program will let you know. This will identify contact details that may have changed, much like the duplicates do. You can then examine and approve them as necessary.

When Changes Are Undone

You are responsible for any mistakes you make when editing your contacts. This is so that you can restore your contacts to any previous state within the last 30 days using Google Contacts. To undo changes, all you have to do is click the setting icon located in the upper right corner of the screen. The system prompts you to select the time you want to return to.

Your Directory Of Contacts

You will notice an option on the left-hand side of the bar if your company uses GSuite, which includes Gmail and Google Contacts. The directory that is your own Google Contacts account does not have this option. Your email addresses in the domain of your company are included in your directory, which is only a list of users. This implies that Google can arrange a meeting with anyone in your organization, regardless of whether you have previously emailed them or not, and it can also automatically fill in your coworkers' email addresses. The email addresses that are listed in the directory are determined by the system administrator. Additionally, they may always take contacts out of it.

Interface Contacts

Beginning in March 2015, Google began testing a new user interface. You can visit contacts.google.com/preview to view a preview of their redesigned Google Contacts web interface. Launched in 2015, this preview has already built their new interface as of 2021. Compared to its previous interface, this new one seems superior. In 2016, they released a somewhat modified version for G Suite subscribers.

The Interesting Onboarding

Users will now be able to gather all of their contact information from Google thanks to their new onboarding process. This causes the card to show the data that you typically enter by hand, together with the information that each contact has shared on their Google profile. It also provides a brief explanation of how it manages duplicates.

Image Of The Primary Interface

The redesigned Google Contacts utilizes Indigo, which features a large search inbox and a title bar. The primary contact list avatars are in a left column. You may access frequently contacted individuals, duplicates, labels, and settings through its concealed side column. Numerous choices are available, including import, export, print, and undo modifications. If you'd like to revert to the previous version, it allows you to do so. You can now navigate through the complete contact list without having to flip between pages like you used to. A contact can be highlighted to reveal several options, such as the overflow menu, edit, and favorite. You can even choose multiple contacts to merge them. They can be hidden or deleted, labeled, and even emailed together. There is no longer a contacts per page selection, and the settings have somewhat modified. It is not possible to turn off keyboard shortcuts.

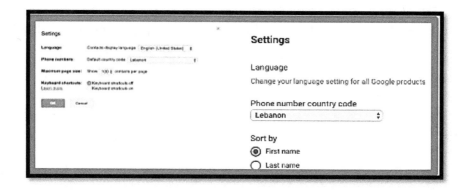

By default, their keyboard shortcuts are activated, so all you have to do is tap to see them. To navigate from the left column to your contact list, there are no arrows. You can now add a new contact creation card, which overlaps the main list, by clicking the floating Fuschia action button at the bottom right of the screen. The identical issue arises each time you open a contact info. The card overlaps rather than opens on a new page, and you can see that the interface describes each field with an icon rather than a word. All of the contact information you typically enter for each person is displayed on the card. Additionally, you will discover all the information you submitted to their Google

194

profile as well as the history of your interactions with them, such as emails and shared events. You'll also note that the contacts' actions have altered. This gives you the option to modify the labels attached to a contact or to conceal or remove them. It is not possible to print, export, or even select to display your other data.

Last but not least, the 2015 preview interface included information on each contact in four columns, with each contact's email address, phone number, physical address, and labels displayed next to their names. The email address, phone number, job title, and firm are displayed in three columns on the new interface.

About Labels

The most intriguing feature of the Google apps is this. After months of delay, Google began adding app privacy labels in February. Using Gmail as an example, it launched its app privacy label on February 22nd, and over time, its other apps received gradual updates. While Google updated its main app with app privacy details by adding information to their Google pictures, other applications, like Google Maps, secretly updated their privacy settings just last week. On December 8, 2020, Google started enforcing their app privacy label. The purpose of the app privacy labels is to notify you about everything related to the app and its access, not the data that the app will access. For instance, suppose an application is limited to using location data solely while displaying a map to you. In any case, the privacy label often doesn't indicate that; instead, it's simply a used/not used binary.

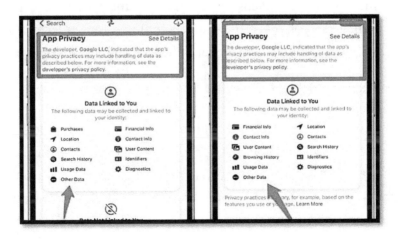

Contact Import And Export

Importing and exporting contacts to Google is crucial. Transferring your crucial data that is saved on Google Apps is much simpler. The purpose of the data transfer is irrelevant, regardless of whether you want to send data to or from your account. You may occasionally need to share contacts, data, or contact groups with another Google account as an online or internet user. You could wish to move your contacts from your personal Gmail account to your business Google Apps account, or you might want to share your critical contact group with a friend or coworker. In any case, all you need to know is that importing and exporting all of your Goole contacts is really easy.

To export and import contacts:

You must first log into your Gmail account before clicking the mail button, which is located on the left side of the bar. To view your Gmail message list instead of the Contact manager, which is located in the center of the screen, select Contacts. Click on the App grid and choose Contacts after opening the contact manager in a new Chrome tab. Choose Export from the list by clicking the More button at the top of the screen. You can choose the contacts you wish to export from the new window that appears. If you would like to export every contact, you can choose every contact. To choose just one contact group, choose the group you want from the list that is arranged top-down. You can choose the export format you wish to use while in the window. Here, I've chosen the Google CSV format. When you wish to import your contacts back into your other Google account, this is the best option. Please note that you must click Export after selecting "Outlook CSV Format" if you need to import contacts to Outlook, Yahoo, or even Hotmail, or "vCard Format" if you want to import contacts to your Apple address book.

Importing Gmail Contact Details

To access your Gmail account, you must sign in. After selecting Contacts from the menu that appears in the left sidebar, you can see the contact manager in the center of the screen, which has taken the place of the Gmail message list. Next Click on the Apps grid, open the Contact Manager in a new Chrome browser tab, and choose Contacts. The next step is to import Contacts, which may be found in the left sidebar. Once the processes to export contacts from the other account are complete, click Choose File and select the location where you saved your.csv file. After choosing the file, select Open. The following step is to select Import. Your import will then be finished, and your contact group will have the name "Imported."

How To Print

The steps to print from your Google app are as follows:

- Navigate to your computer's desktop and choose the Google Chrome logo.

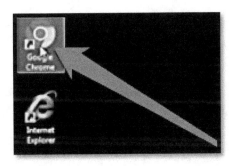

It will bring you to the Google page

Next, type www.google.com as shown below,

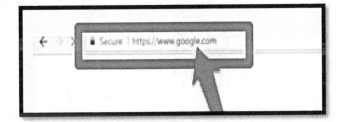

Then go to the top right-hand corner where there is three-dot and click.

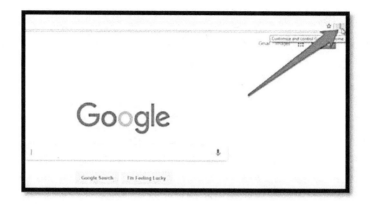

When you click on your menu button, it will display the menu and then move the arrow cursor and click on print as shown below.

Wait for the print preview page to load.

Make sure you have the right printer by going to have a look at the left top bar.

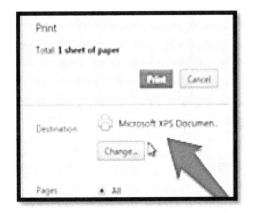

Check where the destination is on the left top bar and click on the change as shown in the screenshot below

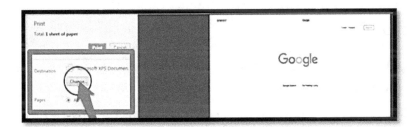

Choose from the list of printers that are stored on the computer

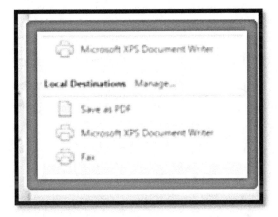

At the bottom of the left-hand bar, you can choose the layout of your print, whether you want a portrait or landscape. You can choose the colour of your print also.

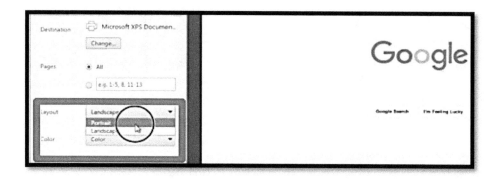

After making those adjustments, select Print to have your document printed out.

Final Summary

This book covers a great deal of ground when it comes to Google Apps. Google Apps have completely changed the online landscape, with very few people using the internet these days without utilizing Google Apps. In the webmail industry, Google has surpassed industry titans like Yahoo, Hotmail, and others. There is a lot of discussion about whether Google will surpass Microsoft with its Google Docs, which many businesses now favor because they enable data sharing and other collaborations between employees and their employers as well as numerous other activities involving the sharing of individual and corporate accounts with friends, family, and coworkers. Since Google Docs' introduction in the online business world, it has facilitated worldwide cooperation between individuals and corporations, and its data sharing feature has given it an advantage over Microsoft.

You can even use Google Docs offline, and it offers you amazing opportunities. With word processors, spreadsheets, presentations, reading, writing, storing emails, and scheduling and meeting capabilities—all of which are quite useful—Google Apps products are going to overtake Microsoft in the near future. While writing this book, I discovered several benefits that might propel Google to the top; things that nobody ever imagined were conceivable are now made possible by Google. Google Apps introduced web browser-based capabilities for productivity, communication, and teamwork. The fact that the majority of Google's App programs are available for free is by far the most remarkable and intriguing feature of Google and its offerings. Google designed their software so that you may use their word processor, spreadsheet, email, chat, and web page builder for free without having to pay a single cent. Though the majority of

Google's apps are available for free, there are those that are paid for. They refer to their premium edition as a premier edition. Unlike their 2GB free email storage, the premier version allows you greater access to their other applications, such as their 10 GB email storage.

Applications for word processing, spreadsheet work, presentation creation, email reading, writing, and archiving, appointment scheduling, and more are all included in the Google Apps suite. Google Apps enabled online browser-based collaboration, productivity, and communication solutions. The fact that the majority of Google App programs are free to use is really intriguing. Word processing, spreadsheets, email, chat, Web page builder, and more are all available without costing you a single cent. In addition to the Google App's free version, there is a premium edition that you can purchase called the premier edition. Unlike the free edition, which only offers 2GB of email storage, the premier edition gives you access to more programs and offers 10GB of email storage. Additionally, a 99.9% email uptime guarantee is provided to elite users. In addition, the premium edition offers you the option to block contextual ads on Google services and round-the-clock phone support. You also receive customized advanced features for your business in addition to these. Although I can't cover everything in this conclusion, I will predict that Google will unexpectedly surpass industry giants like Microsoft in the near future. This is just my own prediction; you may have different ideas. However, I can guarantee you that this book has been very beneficial.